BEYOND THE ASTERISK

BEYOND THE ASTERISK

Understanding Native Students
in Higher Education

EDITED BY

Heather J. Shotton, Shelly C. Lowe,
and Stephanie J. Waterman

Foreword by John L. Garland

STERLING, VIRGINIA

COPYRIGHT © 2013 BY
STYLUS PUBLISHING, LLC.

Published by Stylus Publishing, LLC
22883 Quicksilver Drive
Sterling, Virginia 20166-2102

Library of Congress Cataloging-in-Publication Data
Beyond the asterisk : understanding Native students in
higher education / edited by Heather Shotton, Shelly Lowe,
and Stephanie J. Waterman.
   p. cm.
Includes bibliographical references and index.
ISBN 978-1-57922-623-7 (cloth : alk. paper)
ISBN 978-1-57922-624-4 (pbk. : alk. paper)
ISBN 978-1-57922-625-1 (library networkable e-edition)
ISBN 978-1-57922-626-8 (consumer e-edition)
1. Indians of North America—Education (Higher)—United
States.   2. Indian students—United States.   I. Shotton,
Heather, 1976–
E97.B49   2013
378.1'98297—dc23   2012040238

13-digit ISBN: 978-1-57922-623-7 (cloth)
13-digit ISBN: 978-1-57922-624-4 (paper)
13-digit ISBN: 978-1-57922-625-1 (library networkable
e-edition)
13-digit ISBN: 978-1-57922-626-8 (consumer e-edition)

Printed in the United States of America

All first editions printed on acid-free paper
that meets the American National Standards Institute
Z39-48 Standard.

Bulk Purchases

Quantity discounts are available for use in workshops
and for staff development.
Call 1-800-232-0223

First Edition, 2013

10   9   8   7   6   5   4   3   2   1

To the professionals of IPKC and NAN
who have supported this work
and who will continue the research and work after.

CONTENTS

ACKNOWLEDGMENTS

We would like to express our deepest gratitude to the authors who contributed to this book who include Native scholars, practitioners, professionals, and our non-Native allies. Each of them shares his or her knowledge of Native students, their experiences, expertise, and wisdom. In conceptualizing this book, it was important to us that it be written from a Native perspective and give voice to Native professionals and scholars in higher education. Our knowledge, experience, perspectives, and values as Native people are embedded into each chapter. To Dr. Donna Brown, Dr. Charlotte Davidson, Dr. Timothy Ecklund, Karen Francis-Begay, Dr. John Garland, Dr. Justin Guillory, Freida Jacques, Steven Martin, Dr. George McClellan, Dr. Robin Minthorn, Derek Oxendine, Symphony Oxendine, CHiXapkaid (Dr. D. Michael Pavel), Dr. Cornel Pewewardy, Molly Springer, Amanda Tachine, Danielle Terrance, Adrienne Thunder, your contributions to this book are invaluable; without each of you and your vision, this book would not have been possible. We also want to thank Pamela Kaptein, Timothy Argetsinger, and Thomas Krause for their information gathering, formatting assistance, and general input. We say *ahe'hee'*, *ah-ho day-own-day*, and *nya weñha*; thank you, it is good.

THANKSGIVING

As Haudenosaunee (Iroquois to most), our first duty is to give thanks. So this is how we will begin this effort as well.

Let us remember and give Thanksgiving and Respect to all Humanity. We would be lost without our families, our husbands, wives, life partners, children, aunts, uncles, and grandparents. We enjoy our communities, our towns, our cities, and our Nations. They make our lives rich in love.

Let us send Thanksgiving and Respect to our Mother, the Earth. She has sustained us from the beginning and is consistent in her nurturing ways.

Let us send Thanksgiving and Respect to all the Waters on Mother Earth: from the tiny fresh water springs, the creeks, the rivers, and on to the great saltwater oceans. All life depends on water. We also remember and thank all the life that lives in the water, which includes great nations of fish.

Let us send Thanksgiving and Respect to all the Medicines that grow on Mother Earth. We are thankful that they continue to grow in the fields and the woodlands. They are used by our medicine people to help keep our Nations healthy.

We send Thanksgiving and Love to all the Berries that grow in the fields. They act as medicine and help lighten our spirits and give us joy when we pick and eat them. The strawberry, blackberry, raspberry, and blueberry are only a few of the many berries we enjoy on Mother Earth.

We send Thanksgiving, Love, and Respect to all the Tree-Life on Mother Earth. They provide warmth to our homes, utensils, syrup, fruit, medicine, and oxygen and great beauty. Anyone who has driven through the northeast in the fall has gasped at the beauty of the trees. The Cottonwood in the west can be a bright, bright yellow. The great canopies of South America nurture wonders of bird-life, medicine, and creatures of all kinds.

We send Thanksgiving, Love, and Respect to all the free-running Animals on Mother Earth. We would be sad if we did not get to see the raccoon, or the deer, or the fox run by our homes. There are many, many wild and free animals on earth, and we are thankful for them all.

We are Thankful for all the Life-giving Food on Mother Earth. We have depended on the corn, the beans, and squash for millennia in our territories. But all food that keeps you alive is good food, so we remember and send Thanksgiving to all the Food on Mother Earth.

We send Greetings, Love, and Respect to all the Bird-Life. They travel across the earth and remind us of the seasons as they change. We hear their beautiful songs in the springtime. The songs lift our spirits. The geese fly by and remind us of how we need to work together as they do.

We send Thanksgiving to the Winds of the four directions. They come and clear the air, so we have clean air to breath. The northern winds come and bring the cool weather and remind the trees and all plant life that it is time to rest. The warm winds come from the south to waken them, and we see the spring flowers and the wonderful greenery of summer.

We remember the Thunder Beings and send them Thanksgiving, Love, and Respect. They bring the rains that help all the green plants grow. Our gardens depend on the rain. All life depends on a consistent supply of water, and we depend on the Thunder Beings to come and replenish our supply.

We send Greetings, Respect, and Love to our Elder Brother, the Sun. He is constant in his movement across the sky. His rays send energy to all the greenery on Earth and they thrive because of it. We have the light that shines on earth from our Elder Brother, the Sun, and we can see one another and all the beauty of Earth because of him.

We send Love, Respect, and Greetings to our Grandmother Moon. Her beauty in the sky is breathtaking. She guides the ocean tides. She guides all the females on Earth so that there may be new life.

With our Grandmother Moon we see the beauty of all the Stars in the Sky. We send Greetings, Love, and Respect to the Stars for they fulfill their duties given to them by Creator. Their beauty lifts our hearts with joy.

As you think of these that we have given Thanksgiving to, you may be reminded of another part of Creation that was left out. Please feel free to give thanks to it as well.

In this modern era, many are busy running about with their business, and most, when they stop to be thankful, think of only the things they have acquired. It is easy when you are busy to take for granted the many parts of Creation that we depend on each day. We are fortunate to be living on Earth when the climates are welcoming to Human Life.

I remember how I felt when I first understood the warnings about Global warming. It was a feeling of loss and mourning. Those places on Earth that man took hundreds of years to study would soon be much, much different from what we have become accustomed to expect. In the near future, it is very likely we will travel to the Arctic and it will not be a white frozen land, and the Polar Bear will be scarce, having lost his habitat.

Stop and reflect, what do humans offer the Earth? What is their part in this interconnected plan? If any of these parts of Creation stop doing their duty, how would it affect human life? The truth is that we are consumers. We thrive only because we can count on the other parts of Creation. We are fortunate to have our habitat on Earth, and we need to continue to give Thanks for all of her wonders.

Now, we can continue on to other business.

Freida J. Jacques, Onondaga, Turtle Clan
Onondaga, January 11, 2011

FOREWORD

Dr. John L. Garland (Choctaw)

H*alito*! This is indeed a historic moment in the development of higher education. Within this important and much-anticipated addition to the literature, higher education faculty and administrators have important new resources for helping shift the landscape of Native American college student experiences toward success. Not since the seminal 2005 edition of the *New Directions for Student Services* series, titled *Serving Native American Students*, has higher education had such a comprehensive resource on this topic. The importance of this particular text cannot be understated. It has been conceived, written, and edited by Native American higher education leaders and those who have made Native students a priority in their practice.

During the first few years of my doctoral course work at the University of Maryland, I became increasingly frustrated with the invisibility of Native American representation in the student development literature. In 2004 I began focusing my research presentations at national student affairs conferences on the Native American research "asterisk" phenomenon by identifying major gaps in the literature and proposing specific research agendas to address these gaps. While progress has been made since that time, there is much more work left to do. Today, when I meet colleagues and higher education administrators at conferences and meetings, there seems to be an overwhelming consensus that Native American college student invisibility is no longer acceptable in the literature or on campus. The next logical step seems to be finding ways of taking action, and this book is, indeed, a tool for action. The critical questions for higher education administrators and researchers from this point forward are: *Why has it taken this long, and why was it necessary to primarily rely on Native Americans to make this contribution in an era of widespread expectations for cultural competence and diversity initiatives in higher education?* and *From this point forward, will higher education collectively accept responsibility for removing the Native American asterisk in the research literature and within student, faculty, and staff campus representation?*

With *Beyond the Asterisk: Understanding Native Students in Higher Education*, the editors and authors have provided the higher education community with a solid foundation for responding to the needs of our Native students. In fact, many of the contributors are products of colleges and universities where Native students are often invisible, and yet these authors succeeded in spite of the quantitative odds. These examples of Native student success are too often the exception instead of the rule. This text renders *visible* all Native Americans in higher education (students, faculty, and staff). My hope is that this book becomes a catalyst for new higher education practices that lead to direct and increased support for Native Americans and others who are working vigorously to remove the Native American asterisk from research and practice. This text also signals a renewed call to action for increasing the representation of Native students, faculty, and staff on our campuses that was originally sounded by higher education visionaries Vine Deloria Jr., Ernest Boyer, Paul Boyer, William Tierney, and many others.

I am very proud of my Native colleagues, Heather J. Shotton, Shelly C. Lowe, and Stephanie J. Waterman, for taking on this critical project. Along with the chapter authors, they are outstanding examples of higher education's Native leaders and allies affecting positive change for our colleges and universities and, most important, for *all* students.

Yakoke.

INTRODUCTION

Dr. Heather J. Shotton (Wichita/Kiowa/Cheyenne), Shelly C. Lowe (Diné), and Dr. Stephanie J. Waterman (Onondaga, Turtle)

An important aspect of higher education and the student affairs profession is understanding the students we serve. Unfortunately, general understanding of the Native American population in higher education is severely lacking. The lack of knowledge and understanding about this particular population may be attributed to our invisibility within the academy. In the past 30 years, the number of Native Americans attending postsecondary institutions has more than doubled (National Center for Education Statistics [NCES], 2005). However, Native American enrollment and retention in institutions of higher education remain the lowest compared to other populations.

While enrollment of Native Americans in postsecondary institutions has increased, Native Americans remain grossly underrepresented in postsecondary education. It has been reported that Native Americans make up only 1% of the total college student population (Aud, Hussar, Kena, Bianco, Frohlich, Kemp, & Tahan, 2011; Snyder, Tan, & Hoffman, 2004), despite the current trends of increased enrollment. Furthermore, data confirm that attrition rates are disproportionately high for Native Americans and that Native American students are the least likely to graduate from college (Benjamin, Chambers, & Reiterman, 1993; NCES, 2005; Pavel, 1999; Reddy, 1993). The issues, needs, and characteristics of this population are multifaceted and unique. Understanding student success, development, and learning, particularly with regard to culturally relevant and inclusive models, is at the core of the student affairs profession. Unfortunately, the current literature is almost silent with regard to these issues among Native American students in higher education. Recent review of two well-known student affairs association journals, the *Journal of College Student Development* and *NASPA Journal* (now the *Journal of Student Affairs Research and Practice*) from 1991 to 2011, revealed that only 1.5% had Native American or American Indian in the title or abstract (Emery, Sands, Raucci-Youngs, & Waterman, 2011). For student affairs professionals and institutions to serve this population better, they must first understand its needs as well as proven approaches to serving Native American students (Lin, LaCounte, & Eder, 1988; Pavel & Padilla, 1993; Wells, 1997).

In 2007 a group of Native higher education professionals and scholars gathered at the University of Illinois–Urbana-Champaign to discuss Native students in higher education and ways to better serve them (many of the authors in this book were present at that meeting). During this gathering the issue of the invisibility of Natives and the lack of a Native voice in higher education literature was discussed. While the *New Directions for Student Services* series monograph, *Serving Native American Students* (Fox, Lowe, & McClellan, 2005), had been released just two years before this meeting, those present recognized that there remained a need for a continued push to make our voices heard and continue the dialogue about understanding Native students in higher education. In fact, Fox and associates (2005) specifically called for continued action to "achieve what is possible in serving and supporting Native American students in higher education" (p. 98); this book is a response to that call for action.

Native scholars and practitioners have long struggled with the invisibility of Native people within the academy; we are often excluded from institutional data and reporting, omitted from the curriculum, absent from the research and literature, and virtually written out of the higher education story. In particular, data on Native American students are generally not reported or discussed in quantitative research findings, or are noted as not statistically significant, which has resulted in a phenomenon that has been referred to as the "American Indian research asterisk" (Garland, 2007, p. 612; Lowe, 2005). The absence of data on Native American students reinforces our invisibility, where our presence is hidden by the ever-present "asterisk," and further marginalizes Native people. Furthermore, the asterisk mentality concerning Natives in academia has resulted in a serious lack of understanding of and dialogue on appropriate solutions. Fryberg and Townsend (2008) explain that invisibility is an intentional act involving an active "writing out" of the story of a particular group, often serving to maintain a status quo that benefits the dominant group (p. 175). The intention of this book is to move beyond the asterisk in an effort to better understand Native students and challenge the status quo.

The value of knowledge about Native Americans extends beyond providing an informed base for practice in higher education. The authors in this book are dedicated to and experienced in Native American student support.

They share the wealth of their experiences so the reader can learn about the Native experience in higher education. Understanding Native epistemologies, culture, and social structures provides a richer array of options through which student affairs professionals and institutions may approach their work and missions. The reader will see that Indigenous epistemologies and knowledge systems are based on relationships. Because most higher education professionals and faculty are non-Native, this book provides needed resources for supporting this population. Over two decades ago, William G. Tierney also made a call for more work "by and for Native Americans about their relationship to the world of higher education" (1990, p. 93). This book explores that relationship.

Throughout this book we explore ways in which higher education professionals and institutions can better understand and, more important, better serve Native students. As our college campuses become more and more diverse, college professionals need a greater array of information about today's students. The Native population in particular is extremely diverse; there are over 560 federally recognized tribal nations (*Federal Register*, 2010) as well as a number of state-recognized tribal nations in the United States. The exact number of state-recognized tribes is difficult to determine, as each state has its own process for recognition, further illuminating the complex nature of tribal governments. Native people live on reservations, in border towns, and in urban areas. Many are traditional, many are not, and many practice their traditions in addition to Christianity. There is no one physical characteristic that sets Native people apart. It must be understood that the daily and historical experiences of Native Americans are diverse and vary from tribe to tribe (Brayboy, Fann, Castagno, & Solyom, 2012). While we explore some of the common experiences of Natives in higher education, we acknowledge that there is not one singular Native experience in higher education. One thing is clear, Native students have not been well served by mainstream institutions, or non-Native colleges and universities (NNCUs), as is evident by current enrollment and graduation statistics (Brayboy et al., 2012). Leaders within higher education, faculty, and professionals must do a better job of understanding our Native students if we are to better serve them.

Definition of Terms

Throughout this book we use terminology that we feel is important to define for our readers.

American Indian/Native American/Native/Indigenous

We use the terms *American Indian, Native American, Native,* and *Indigenous* interchangeably. Each of these terms refers to the Indigenous populations of North America, particularly those located in what we now know as the United States and those who identify as Native American or Alaska Native. This includes those who are members or descendants of both federally and state-recognized tribes. Native people are both political and racialized beings (Brayboy, 2005). It is important to understand that Native people are not just an ethnic minority; rather, our identity is situated within our unique status as members of sovereign nations; hence, we are also recognized as a political group.

Non-Native Colleges and Universities

For this book we chose to use the term *non-Native colleges and universities* (NNCUs) to describe those institutions that represent the predominantly White population, typically referred to as predominantly White institutions (PWIs) or mainstream institutions. The use of the term *NNCU* is a conscious effort to center our experience as Native people.

Tribal Colleges and Universities

The terms *tribal colleges* and *tribal colleges and universities* (TCUs) are used interchangeably throughout this book. TCU refers to those colleges and universities chartered by tribal governments. Tribal identity is at the core of every TCU, and they all share the mission of tribal self-determination and service to their respective communities (American Indian Higher Education Consortium [AIHEC], 2012).

Historically Native Fraternities and Sororities

The term *historically Native American fraternities and sororities* (HNAFS) is used to describe Native American Greek organizations that were founded on the principles of Native American cultural beliefs (Jahansouz & Oxendine, 2008). These organizations resemble some aspects of traditional Greek organizations but are based in tribal and Native American cultural beliefs.

Native American Student Services Unit

The term *Native American Student Services Unit* (NASSU) was developed for this book to refer to student support units specifically for Native American students. Native American Studies Programs are academic programs that typically include student support (Champagne & Stauss, 2002); however, NASSUs are units that stand in partnership with, or separate from, those academic programs. NASSUs are charged with student support often located within an institution's student affairs division.

Natives in Higher Education

Higher education enrollment for Native American students has more than doubled in the last 30 years, increasing from 76,100 in 1976 to 181,100 in 2006 (NCES, 2007). Despite this steady rise in enrollment, Native American college students remain less likely than their peers to enroll in college (DeVoe, Darling-Churchill, & Snyder, 2008). In 2009 Native students constituted 1% of the total undergraduate population in postsecondary institutions (Aud et al., 2011). As demonstrated in Figure I-1, Native students consistently make up the lowest percentage of the population in higher education.

When we examine Native college student enrollment further, it is evident that there is a gender gap in the enrollment rates of Native American males and females: Native American males lag behind Native American females. In 2009 Native American females accounted for approximately 60% (113,000) of the Native American students enrolled in higher education, compared to 40% (77,000) for Native American males (Aud et al., 2011). This is in stark contrast to enrollment rates for Native American males and females almost 30 years ago, when the number of Native American males and females enrolled in college was nearly equal (see Figure I-2) (Aud et al., 2011).

In terms of enrollment patterns for Native American students at various types of institutions, little has changed. Lowe (2005) tells us that "Native Americans continue to be underrepresented both in the more prestigious private and four-year sectors of higher education and over-represented in the less prestigious public and two-year sectors" (p. 34). In 2009, 44.9% of Native American postsecondary students were enrolled in public, two-year institutions (Aud et al., 2011). Moreover, 80% of all Native students enrolled full-time in colleges and universities were in public institutions as opposed to private institutions, and only 5.5% were enrolled in a tribal college (Swail, Redd, & Perna, 2003). Brayboy et al. (2012) explain that the pattern of enrollment of Native students at two-year institutions is related to issues of the proximity of Native students to four-year institutions, high school preparation, and socioeconomic status.

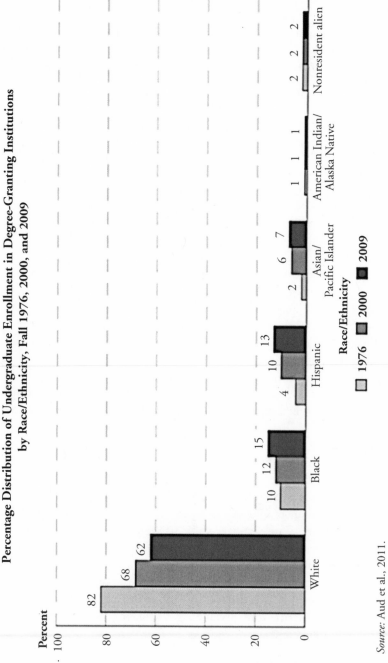

FIGURE I-1
Percentage Distribution of Undergraduate Enrollment in Degree-Granting Institutions by Race/Ethnicity, Fall 1976, 2000, and 2009

Percent

100

80

60

40

20

0

82 68 62 — White

10 12 15 — Black

4 10 13 — Hispanic

2 6 7 — Asian/Pacific Islander

1 1 1 — American Indian/Alaska Native

2 2 2 — Nonresident alien

Race/Ethnicity

☐ 1976   ■ 2000   ■ 2009

Source: Aud et al., 2011.

FIGURE I-2
Number of American Indian/Alaska Native Undergraduates Enrolled in Degree-Granting Institutions, Fall 1976–2009

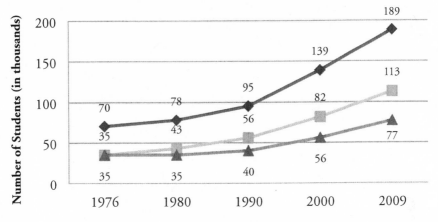

Fall Enrollment Year

◆ Combined   ■ AI/AN Female   ▲ AI/AN Male

Source: Aud et al., 2011.

When we move beyond enrollment patterns and further examine retention and graduation rates of Native American students, it is evident that Native students have some of the lowest retention and graduation rates. Some have noted the complexity of accurately determining precise retention figures for Native students (Boyer, 1997; Carney, 1999; Tierney, 1992). Even so, the range of attrition rates for Native students has been estimated between 75% and 93% (Brown & Robinson Kurpius, 1997). In 2008, 38.3% of Native American students completed a bachelor's degree, the lowest rate of all racial and ethnic groups and well below the national average of 57.2% (Aud et al., 2011). Table I-1 demonstrates the gap in the six-year graduation rate for Native American students compared to non-Native students.

While the overall degree attainment of Native Americans has increased at all degree levels, Native Americans still account for a small percentage of the total number of degrees conferred annually (NCES, 2007). Brayboy et al. (2012) put the underrepresentation of Native graduates into perspective when they explain that "for every one American Indian or Alaska Native who has a bachelor's degree, seven White individuals do" (p. 56).

TABLE I-1
Six-Year Graduation Rates by Race/Ethnicity

Race/ethnicity	*Six-year graduation rate for cohort entering college in 2002*
American Indian/Alaska Native	38.3%
Hispanic	48.9%
African American	40.1%
Asian American/Pacific Islander	67.1%
White	60.2%

Source: Aud et al., 2011.

Native Graduate Students

Participation of Native students in graduate and professional programs has steadily increased over the last 30 years (NCES, 2010). Despite this increase, Native students are still grossly underrepresented in graduate education, constituting only a fraction of a percent (0.6%) of total graduate enrollment. Furthermore, women make up 64% of total graduate enrollment for American Indians/Alaska Natives, compared to 36% for males (Bell, 2011). Table I-2 highlights the enrollment patterns for all racial/ethnic groups in the United States.

While racial/ethnic minority students have driven a great deal of the enrollment increase for first-time graduate students in the United States, Native students recently experienced a drop (Bell, 2011). In the fall of 2010, there was a 20.6% decline in the first-time graduate enrollment and a 10.3% decline in total graduate enrollment (including graduate certificates and master's and doctoral programs) for American Indians/Alaska Natives (Bell, 2011). Based on this low graduate school participation, it is not surprising to find that Native American faculty and staff are also underrepresented.

Native Faculty and Staff

Although women and scholars of color have made inroads into higher education, inequalities still exist, and White men continue to dominate faculty positions in institutions of higher education (Rai & Critzer, 2000). Native

TABLE I-2
Total Graduate Enrollment and Percentage Distribution of Students in Degree-Granting Institutions by Race/Ethnicity, Fall 1976–2009

Race/ethnicity and sex	Enrollment (in thousands)					Percentage distribution of students				
	1976[1]	1980[1]	1990	2000	2009	1976[1]	1980[1]	1990	2000	2009
Total	**1,578**	**1,622**	**1,860**	**2,157**	**2,862**	**99.3**	**99.7**	**100.0**	**100.0**	**100.0**
Race/ethnicity										
White	1,336	1,352	1,450	1,479	1,816	84.7	83.4	78.0	68.6	63.4
African American	90	88	100	181	342	5.7	5.4	5.4	8.4	12.0
Hispanic	31	39	58	111	184	2.0	2.4	3.1	5.1	6.4
Asian/Pacific Islander	29	38	72	133	195	1.8	2.3	3.9	6.2	6.8
American Indian/Alaska Native	6	6	7	13	18	0.4	0.4	0.4	0.6	0.6
Nonresident alien	75	95	173	241	306	4.8	5.9	9.3	11.2	10.7

[1] Race/ethnicity estimates may not sum to totals owing to underreporting and nonreporting of racial/ethnic data.

Source: NCES, 2010.

faculty members are one of the smallest segments of American higher education (Cross, 1991; Turner, González, & Wood, 2011). In the fall of 2009, 0.5% of full-time faculty at colleges and universities identified as American Indian or Alaska Native, compared to 77.3% who identified as White (*Almanac of Higher Education*, 2011).

Moreover, when we examine various faculty ranks further, Natives are grossly underrepresented among assistant, associate, and full professors. According to Trower and Chait (2002), African American, Hispanic, and Native American faculty constitute only 5% of the full professors in the United States. In 2009 Native American faculty were least represented (0.3%) at the full professor level (*Almanac of Higher Education*, 2011). Table I-3 illustrates representation of full-time faculty by race.

The role of Native faculty in the success of Native students has long been noted (Brown & Robinson Kurpius, 1997; Falk & Aitken, 1984; Swisher, Hoisch, & Pavel, 1991; Terenzini, Pascarella, & Blimling, 1996; Wright, 1985). Recently, Brayboy et al. (2012) articulated the critical role that Native faculty play, not just for Native students, but for tribal communities as well:

> Native faculty serve as activists, advocates, and change agents in postsecondary institutions and in their disciplines by challenging dominant, racist, and discriminatory scholarship, practices and perceptions; by stimulating research in Indigenous issues; by developing and infusing curriculum that is inclusive of Native perspectives and scholarship; by assisting colleges and universities in recruiting and retaining Native students; and through networking with Native organizations. (p. 93)

Just as Native faculty play a pivotal role in the success of Native students in higher education, so do Native staff members.

Although the participation numbers of Native staff members are not as low as the numbers representing faculty participation, they are again the lowest of all reported racial groups. Native Americans in professional staff and executive/administrative/managerial positions make up only 0.5% of the total population, and those in nonprofessional staff positions make up only 0.8% of the total population (NCES, 2010). The total proportion of Native American staff in all institutions is only 0.6% (NCES, 2010). As you will see in this book, supporting Native American students in higher education requires taking a good look at how both Native faculty and staff are being supported, and finding opportunities for them to participate at higher rates.

TABLE I-3

Percentage of Full-Time Faculty in Degree-Granting Institutions, Fall 2009

Academic rank	White	Black	Latino	API	AI/AN
Professor	85.1	3.5	2.7	7.6	0.3
Associate professor	80.0	5.6	3.7	8.6	0.4
Assistant professor	70.6	6.6	4.1	11.2	0.4
Instructor	77.5	7.7	6.5	5.5	1.0
Lecturer	76.7	5.6	4.9	7.1	0.4
Other faculty	70.3	5.4	3.4	8.0	8.0

Source: Almanac of Higher Education, 2011.

In addition to terminology, demographics, and statistics, it is important to understand the historical context of formal education imposed on Indigenous populations of the Americas and responses to it.

History of Native Education in the United States

Efforts by the Spanish to formally educate the Indigenous people of the Western hemisphere began as early as the 1500s (Wright, 1988). In the 1600s plans to build a college for Native people were discussed in what is now Virginia (Carney, 1999). In 1650 Harvard's charter was "rewritten to include" the education of Native youth after the Society for the Propagation of the Gospel established the Boyle Fund targeting Native people (Carney, 1999, p. 25). Various treaties and legislation, such as the Northwest Ordinance, included educational provisions for Native people. However, education was interpreted through a European lens, not recognizing the Indigenous knowledge systems already in place. Educational policy became one of "kill the Indian in him, and save the man" (Adams, 1995, p. 52), and its purpose was to replace Native culture with White Christian values as a tool for removal to obtain land (Adams, 1988; Carney, 1999). Native children were taken from their homes, sometimes willingly, to attend boarding schools that inculcated a Christian, vocational education. Children were abused and lacked food and comfort; many ran away, while many others became ill and died (Adams, 1995). These boarding schools were run not by Native American communities but by the church and federal government (Adams, 1995) and are not to be confused with tribal colleges or the tribal college movement. Today, many Native college students have a parent or grandparent who attended one of these schools. This is a legacy from which our students experience education.

Sovereignty and Self-Determination

Tribal sovereignty refers to the inherent sovereignty of tribal nations and their right to self-governance, self-determination, and self-education (Lomawaima, 1999; Lomawaima & McCarty, 2002). The U.S. government signed legally binding agreements with American Indian tribes, called treaties (Horse, 2005), which confirm their legal and political status in this country. Although not all tribes have legal treaties with the U.S. government, legislation such as the Indian Reorganization Act of 1934 and federal recognition grant tribes the authority to self-governance and provide for a government-to-government relationship with the United States. A part of self-governance necessarily includes the right to determine the best avenues for educating tribal members; tribes exercise this through self-determination.

Self-determination refers to the rights of tribal nations to determine what is best for, and provide services to, their citizens through self-governance. More simply stated, self-determination means "letting Indian people determine their own destiny through their tribal governments" (Reyhner & Eder, 2004, p. 251). The self-determination era for tribes culminated with the passage of two major pieces of legislation: the Indian Education Act of 1972 and the Indian Self-Determination and Education Assistance Act of 1975 (P.L. 93-638). This period marked a major transition away from the federal government's previous assimilation and termination policies that had proved detrimental to Native people. The Indian Self-Determination and Education Assistance Act allowed tribes to reclaim educational processes in an effort to better address the unique needs of their members and communities (Brayboy et al., 2012). More important, it provided greater control to tribal governments over services and programs (such as education) for tribal members and allowed tribal nations to determine what was best for their own citizens. The self-determination era ushered us into a period of tribal control of education.

Tribal Colleges and Universities

TCUs, which emerged over 40 years ago as a part of the "self-determination movement" (AIHEC, 1999, p. A2), were created in direct response to the needs of Native American students and to serve geographically isolated populations that otherwise had no access to postsecondary education (AIHEC, 1999). The first TCU, Navajo Community College (now Diné College), was established in 1968, and between 1968 and 1978, 16 more TCUs were established (Reyhner & Eder, 2004). In 1978 Congress passed the Tribally Controlled Community College Assistance Act (P.L. 95-471) to provide funding to TCUs, and today, there are 37 TCUs in the United States (AIHEC, 2012).

The core mission and identity of TCUs can be described as nation building, the rebuilding of Indigenous nations through the teaching of tribal histories, language, and culture (Crazy Bull, 2009). The proliferation of TCUs emerged out of a deliberate response of American Indian people to reclaim their cultural heritage and undo the damaging effects of colonization (Boyer, 1997; Horse, 2005). The tribal college movement is driven by the ideals of self-determination and tribal sovereignty to promote the prosperity of tribal communities for future generations (Boyer, 1997; Stein, 2009). Over the past

40 years, significant progress has been made in the tribal college movement. In spite of their humble beginnings, TCUs are growing stronger each year and now serve more than 30,000 American Indian students nationwide (American Indian College Fund [AICF], 2010). Although most TCUs offer two-year degrees, an increasing number now offer baccalaureate and master's degrees (Stein, 2009). TCUs achieved land-grant status in 1994 and have become leaders in areas such as culturally relevant teaching and learning practices and place-based education, and are engaging in research using methodologies and practices that directly benefit tribal communities.

While the authors of this book recognize the vital role TCUs play in higher education for Native people, we have chosen to focus on Native students at NNCUs. It is estimated that 8% of all Native college students are enrolled in TCUs (Freeman & Fox, 2005), meaning that the majority of Native students continue to be enrolled in NNCUs. TCUs are experiencing great success and have a unique understanding of how to serve Native students, and we feel strongly that there needs to be a deeper understanding of serving Native students at NNCUs. A review of recent literature follows.

Current Literature

In the spring of 2005, a seminal collection focused on supporting Native American students in higher education was published as part of the *New Directions in Student Services* monograph series. This monograph, edited by Mary Jo Tippeconnic Fox, Shelly C. Lowe, and George S. McClellan, was the first collection of works by Native authors and experts who have spent years working in support of Natives in higher education. From this collection came a number of recommendations, including most specifically the need for further research and teaching on the experiences of Native Americans in higher education at all levels, and the need to include the voices and expertise of Natives themselves, as well as the unique cultural understandings and epistemologies found in Native cultures. This monograph served as a starting point in the conversation and focused on improving the success and experiences of Native American students, faculty, and staff.

Native Student Retention

Native student retention has been explored by a number of scholars and for many years focused primarily on the failure of Native students. Previous literature identified factors contributing to Native student attrition, such as the lack of academic preparation, cultural conflict or discontinuity, financial difficulties, and difficulty adjusting to university life (Deyhle, 1992; Falk & Aitken, 1984; Huffman, Sill, & Brokenleg, 1986; Lin, 1985; Lin et al., 1988; Scott, 1986; Wells, 1997). More recent literature has turned the focus to factors that facilitate success for Native students. Scholars have identified factors such as family support, structured support systems, supportive faculty and staff, self-efficacy, connection to culture, and connections to home as positive influences on Native student persistence (Brown & Robinson Kurpius, 1997; Dodd, Garcia, Meccage, & Nelson, 1995; Falk & Aitken, 1984; Hoover & Jacobs, 1992; Jackson & Smith, 2001; Jackson, Smith, & Hill, 2003; McInerney & Swisher, 1995; Shotton, Oosahwe, & Cintrón, 2007; Waterman, 2007).

Conventional conversations on retention, integration theories in particular, have generally focused on the college experience of students in isolation from their family or community. In fact, Tinto's (1975, 1986, 1993) model of student departure implies that, to be successful and integrate into college, students must detach from their community. Tierney (1992) later criticized Tinto's model for its failure to account for Native American cultural perspectives. Retention models have been designed largely with mainstream perspectives, certainly lacking Native American viewpoints. Recently though, a retention model based in Indigenous epistemology has emerged to better explain Native student retention.

Building on the concept of family, HeavyRunner and DeCelles (2002) offered a unique voice to the conventional retention conversation by creating a culturally based Family Education Model. This model focuses on the community-based experiences of Native students and their extended families, and encourages institutions to re-create the structure of the extended family prevalent in many Native communities in an effort to enhance Native students' sense of belonging. HeavyRunner and DeCelles (2002) argue that maintaining a sense of family in the college setting reinforces academic persistence for Native students.

Cultural Identity

A recurring theme in the literature on Native students in higher education is that of culture. Culture has been approached from various perspectives, and scholars have discussed at length issues of cultural differences, cultural discontinuity, and cultural identity for Native students. Cultural discontinuity, when the values and culture of Native students are at odds with those of the institution, often pushes Native students out of institutions (Benjamin et al., 1993; Huffman, 2001, 2010; Reyhner, 1992). Put more succinctly, when a Native student enters an NNCU, that student encounters a disruptive cultural experience (Tierney, 1992).

However, other scholars have argued that a strong connection to culture may contribute to academic success (Brayboy, 2004, 2005; Deyhle, 1995; Huffman, 2001, 2003, 2010; Jackson & Smith, 2001; Kirkness & Barnhardt, 1991; Waterman, 2007). In terms of cultural identity, Jackson and Smith (2001) and Huffman (2003, 2010) affirmed that Native Americans can, and should, draw upon their cultural identity to succeed, and resist the notion that their culture is an impediment to their academic success. Waterman (2007) further explains that successful Haudenosaunee students "remained centered in their culture, community, and family—they maintained their cultural integrity" (p. 31). In either respect, culture is a central aspect of the college experience for Native students.

Campus Climate

Campus climate refers to how students perceive the overall institutional environment. Researchers such as Astin (1993), Pascarella and Terenzini (1991, 2005), and González (2002) have developed theoretical models demonstrating the impact institutional environment has on student persistence. The most important factor in the student-institution fit is creating a campus community in which all students feel connected; Hurtado and Carter (1996) describe this as a sense of belonging. Perceived campus environment is a central feature in the academic experience of all students. It has been argued that students of color often experience marginality more frequently than they feel included in institutions of higher education (Pewewardy & Frey, 2004). Research has shown that students of color have a more nuanced perception of campus climate and are more sensitive to various forms of discrimination and prejudice (Ancis, Sedlacek, & Mohr, 2000; Hurtado, Milem, Clayton-Pedersen, & Allen, 1996). Native students often feel isolated and perceive campuses at NNCUs as hostile, pointing to experiences with both active and passive racism (Jackson et al., 2003; Lin et al., 1988; Perry, 2002; Shotton, 2008). The perception of NNCUs as hostile environments for Native students has also been echoed by a number of scholars (Benjamin et al., 1993; Jackson et al., 2003; Kirkness & Barnhardt, 1991; Lin et al., 1988; Woodcock & Alawiye, 2001; Wright, 1990).

Higher Education and Nation Building for Natives

Recently, Brayboy et al. (2012) explored Native higher education in terms of nation building and self-determination. In the monograph, entitled *Postsecondary Education for American Indian and Alaska Natives: Higher Education for Nation Building and Self-Determination*, the authors explore the state of higher education for Native people and provide a comprehensive overview of the factors that influence college access, enrollment, and completion. They also address the experiences of Indigenous students at all levels, as well as those of Indigenous faculty. Most important, Brayboy et al. (2012) focus their discussion of higher education on the themes of nation building, self-determination, and tribal sovereignty, offering important insight into the critical role higher education plays for Native people. The authors argue that tribes must develop "independence of mind" and reclaim Indigenous knowledge systems to assert their sovereignty and begin the process of nation building (p. 15).

Brayboy et al. (2012) draw on the work of several scholars (Cornell & Kalt, 1992; Frickey, 1997; Helton, 2003/2004; Jorgensen, 2007) to offer a definition of tribal nation building that includes not only economic strength but also the "legal/political, cultural, economic, health/nutrition, and education aspects" of national building (p. 12). The authors further posit that education, particularly higher education, is a necessary component of tribal nation building. In explaining the role of education in tribal nation building, the authors state, "In a modern-day society, and accounting for globalization and economic notions of nation building, in order for a tribe to be economically and politically successful, it must also be educationally successful" (p. 27). Furthermore, the authors assert the notion that culturally responsive approaches to education work to ensure educational success, and they urge postsecondary institutions to develop a deeper understanding of tribal sovereignty, self-determination, nation building, and Indigenous knowledge systems to promote the success of Native students so they can serve their tribal communities.

Organization of the Book

Our book is organized by placing first those who drive our work and our passion: students. The first four chapters deal with our work with and understanding of Native student experiences. Chapter 1 discusses the first-year experience from a Native perspective. In this chapter, Amanda Tachine and Karen Francis-Begay examine the experiences of first-year Native students and the role of a Native living/learning community in student retention. In chapter 2, Steven C. Martin and Adrienne L. Thunder discuss the importance of incorporating culture into student programming for Native students. They explore the unique cultural needs of Native students and offer a model for incorporating culture into all aspects of student programming for Native students. Chapter 3 explores Native-themed residential units. Timothy Ecklund and Danielle Terrance center this chapter on the Haudenosaunee concept of "extending the rafters" to describe ways in which some institutions have provided culturally appropriate residential units that reinforce Native culture. In chapter 4, Derek Oxendine, Symphony Oxendine, and Robin Minthorn discuss the fairly new phenomenon of Native fraternities and sororities, and describe the foundations, obstacles, and role of these organizations for Native students.

We then move to administrative matters in the next three chapters. This section focuses on various aspects of institutional efforts and interactions with Native people. Chapter 5 addresses the emerging role of the special advisor to the president on Native American affairs position. In this chapter, Karen Francis-Begay discusses the evolving role of the special advisor position and offers suggestions on how institutions can work to better serve tribal nations. In chapter 6, Justin Guillory provides insight into TCUs. He examines the distinctive qualities of TCUs and explores the delicate balance of collaborations between NNCUs and TCUs. Chapter 7 introduces the unique emergence and role of NASSUs. Here Molly Springer, Charlotte E. Davidson, and Stephanie J. Waterman describe the multifaceted role of offices that serve Native students and the proximity of such offices to Native American Studies programs.

The book is rounded out in the last section with a focus on how to support Natives in areas beyond undergraduate and administrative areas. CHiXapkaid (Dr. D. Michael Pavel) addresses Native professional and graduate students in chapter 8. He uses his own journey as a graduate student and faculty member to provide recommendations for how institutions can better serve Native students in graduate programs. In chapter 9, Cornel Pewewardy envisions the efforts to increase Indigenous faculty role models as fancy war dancing on the glass ceiling of the academy. He explores the complicated issues of Indigenous role models in higher education and the important role that Indigenous faculty play in student success. Chapter 10 discusses the role of professional associations in assisting student affairs professionals with fulfilling their role of supporting the success of Native American students, staff, and faculty in higher education. In this chapter John L. Garland and George S. McClellan explore the historical roots and contemporary role of national professional organizations and the interaction of such organizations with the Native population. Finally, we conclude with a synthesis of our authors' recommendations and a continued call for institutions to work to better serve Native students and the tribal nations they represent.

References

Adams, D. W. (1988). Fundamental considerations: The deep meaning of Native American schooling, 1880–1900. *Harvard Educational Review, 58*(1), 1–28.

Adams, D. W. (1995). *Education for extinction: American Indians and the boarding school experience: 1875–1928.* Lawrence: University of Press of Kansas.

Almanac of Higher Education. (2011). *Chronicle of Higher Education.* Retrieved March 15, 2012, from http://chronicle.com/article/Almanac-2011-Access-and/128457/

American Indian College Fund (AICF). (2010). *Cultivating success: The critical value of American Indian scholarships and the positive impact of tribal college capital construction.* Retrieved October 1, 2010, from http://www.collegefund.org/userfiles/file/CultivatingSuccess.pdf

American Indian Higher Education Consortium (AIHEC). (1999). *Tribal colleges: An introduction.* Retrieved March 26, 2012, from http://aihec.org/colleges/documents/TCU_intro.pdf

American Indian Higher Education Consortium (AIHEC). (2012, March 26). General format. Retrieved from http://aihec.org/about/historyMission.cfm

Ancis, J. R., Sedlacek, W. E., & Mohr, J. J. (2000). Student perceptions of campus cultural climate by race. *Journal of Counseling & Development, 78*(2), 180–85.

Astin, A. W. (1993). What matters in college? *Liberal Education, 79*(4), 4–15.

Aud, S., Hussar, W., Kena, G., Bianco, K., Frohlich, L., Kemp, J., & Tahan, K. (2011). *The Condition of Education 2011* (NCES 2011-033). Washington, DC: U.S. Department of Education, National Center for Education Statistics.

Bell, N. (2011). *Graduate enrollment and degrees: 2000 to 2010.* Washington, DC: Council of Graduate Schools.

Benjamin, D. P., Chambers, S., & Reiterman, G. (1993). A focus on American Indian college persistence. *Journal of American Indian Education, 32*(2), 24–40.

Boyer, P. (1997). *Native American colleges: Progress and prospects.* Princeton, NJ: Carnegie Foundation for the Advancement of Teaching.

Brayboy, B. M. J. (2004). Hiding in the ivy: American Indian students and visibility in elite educational settings. *Harvard Educational Review, 74*(2), 125–152.

Brayboy, B. M. J. (2005). Toward a tribal critical race theory in education. *The Urban Review, 37*(5), 425–446.

Brayboy , B. M. J., Fann, A. J., Castagno, A. E., & Solyom, J. A. (2012). *Postsecondary education for American Indian and Alaska Natives: Higher education for nation building and self-determination. ASHE Higher Education Report, 37*(5), 1–154. San Francisco: Jossey-Bass.

Brown, L. L., & Robinson Kurpius, S. E. (1997). Psychosocial factors influencing academic persistence of American Indian college students. *Journal of College Student Development, 38*(1), 3–12.

Carney, C. M. (1999). *Native American higher education in the United States.* New Brunswick, NJ: Transaction Publishers.

Champagne, D., & Stauss, J. (2002). *Native American Studies in higher education: Models for collaboration between universities and indigenous nations.* Walnut Creek, CA: AltaMira.

Cornell, S., & Kalt, J. P. (Eds.) (1992). *What can tribes do? Strategies and institutions in American Indian economic development.* Los Angeles: American Indian Studies Center at the University of California, Los Angeles.

Crazy Bull, C. (2009). Tribal colleges and universities: From where we are to where we might go. In L. S. Warner & G. E. Gipp (Eds.), *Tradition and culture in the millennium: Tribal colleges and universities* (pp. 209–217). Charlotte, NC: Information Age.

Cross, W. T. (1991). Pathway to the professoriate: The American Indian faculty pipeline. *Journal of American Indian Education, 1*(2), 20–23.

DeVoe, J. F., Darling-Churchill, K. E., & Snyder, T. D. (2008). *Status and trends in the education of American Indians and Alaska Natives: 2008.* (NCES 2008-08). Washington, DC: National Center for Education Statistics, Institute of Education Sciences, U.S. Department of Education.

Deyhle, D. (1992). Constructing failure and maintaining cultural identity: Navajo and Ute school leavers. *Journal of American Indian Education, 31,* 24–47.

Deyhle, D. (1995). Navajo youth and Anglo racism: Cultural integrity and resistance. *Harvard Educational Review, 65*(3), 403–444.

Dodd, J. M., Garcia, F. M., Meccage, C., & Nelson, J. R. (1995). American Indian student retention. *NASPA Journal, 33*(1), 72–78.

Emery, K., Sands, T. L., Raucci-Youngs, M., & Waterman, S. J. (2011, April 8). Native American college students: A group forgotten roundtable session. New Orleans, LA: American Educational Research Association.

Falk, D. R., & Aitken, L. P. (1984). Promoting retention among American Indian college students. *Journal of American Indian Education, 23*(2), 24–31.

Federal Register (2010, October 1). 75(190), 60810-60814.

Fox, M. J. T., Lowe, S. C., & McClellan, G. S. (Eds.). (2005). *New directions for student services, serving Native American students* (no. 109). San Francisco: Jossey-Bass.

Freeman, C., & Fox, M. (2005). *Status and trends in the education of American Indians and Alaska Natives* (NCES 2005-108). U.S. Department of Education, National Center for Education Statistics. Washington, DC: U.S. Government Printing Office.

Frickey, P. P. (1997). Adjudication and its discontents: Coherence and conciliation in federal Indian law. *Harvard Law Review, 110*(8), 1754–1784.

Fryberg, S. A., & Townsend, S. S. M. (2008). The psychology of invisibility. In G. Adams, M. Biernat, N. R. Branscombe, C. S. Crandall, & L. S. Wrightsman (Eds.), *Commemorating Brown: The social psychology of racism and discrimination* (pp. 173–193). Washington, DC: American Psychological Association.

Garland, J. L. (2007). [Review of the book Serving Native American Students. New Directions for Student Services]. *Journal of College Student Development, 48*, 612–614.

González, K. P. (2002). Campus culture and the experiences of Chicano students in a predominantly White university. *Urban Education, 37*(2), 193–218.

HeavyRunner, I., & DeCelles, D. (2002). Family education model: Meeting the student retention challenge. *Journal of American Indian Education, 41*(2), 29–37.

Helton, T. (2003/2004). National building in Indian country: The Blackfoot constitutional review. *The Kansas Journal of Law and Public Policy, 13*, 1–57.

Hoover, J. J., & Jacobs, C. C. (1992). A survey of American Indian college students: Perceptions toward their study skills/college life. *Journal of American Indian Education, 32*(1), 21–29.

Horse, P. G. (2005). Native American identity. In M. J. Tippeconnic Fox, S. C. Lowe, & G. S. McClellan (Eds.), *New directions for student services, serving Native American students* (no. 109, pp. 33–40). San Francisco: Jossey-Bass.

Huffman, T. E. (2001). Resistance theory and the transculturation hypothesis as explanations of college attrition and persistence among culturally traditional American Indian students. *Journal of American Indian Education, 40*(3), 1–39.

Huffman, T. E. (2003). A comparison of personal assessments of the college experience among reservation and nonreservation American Indian students. *Journal of American Indian Education, 42*(2), 1–16.

Huffman, T. E. (2010). *Theoretical perspectives on American Indian education: Taking a new look at academic success and the achievement gap.* Lanham, MD: AltaMira.

Huffman, T. E., Sill, M., & Brokenleg, M. (1986). College achievement among Sioux and white South Dakota students. *Journal of American Indian Education, 25*(2), 32–38.

Hurtado, S., & Carter, D. F. (1996). Latino students' sense of belonging in the college community: Rethinking the concept of integration on campus. *College students: The evolving nature of research* (pp. 123–136). Needham Heights, MA: Simon & Schuster Custom Publishing.

Hurtado, S., Milem, J. F., Clayton-Pedersen, A., & Allen, W. R. (1996). Enhancing campus climates for racial/ethnic diversity: Educational policy and practice. In

C. Turner, A. Lising Antonio, M. Garcia, B. Laden, A. Nora, & C. Presley (Eds.), *Racial and ethnic diversity in higher education* (pp. 671–684). Boston: Pearson Custom Publishing.

Jackson, A. P., & Smith, S. A. (2001). Postsecondary transitions among Navajo students. *Journal of American Indian Education, 40*(2), 28–47.

Jackson, A. P., Smith, S. A., & Hill, C. L. (2003). Academic persistence among Native American college students. *Journal of College Student Development, 44*(4), 548–565.

Jahansouz, S., & Oxendine, S. (2008, Spring). The Native American fraternal values movement: Past, present, & future. *Perspectives,* 14.

Jorgensen, M. (2007). *Rebuilding native nations: Strategies for governance and development.* Tucson: University of Arizona Press.

Kirkness, V. J., & Barnhardt, R. (1991). First Nations and higher education: The four r's—respect, relevance, reciprocity, responsibility. *Journal of American Indian Education, 30*(3), 1–15.

Lin, R. L. (1985). The promise and the problems of the Native American student. *Journal of American Indian Education, 25*(1), 6–16.

Lin, R. L., LaCounte, D., & Eder, J. (1988). A study of Native American students in a predominantly white college. *Journal of American Indian Education, 27*(3), 8–15.

Lomawaima, K. T. (1999). The unnatural history of American Indian education. In K. G. Swisher & J. W. Tippeconnic III (Eds.), *Next steps: Research and practice to advance Indian education* (pp. 1–31). Charleston, WV: ERIC Clearinghouse on Rural Education and Small Schools.

Lomawaima, K. T., & McCarty, T. L. (2002). When tribal sovereignty challenges democracy: American Indian education and the democratic ideal. *American Educational Research Journal, 39*(2), 279–305.

Lowe, S. C. (2005). This is who I am: Experience of Native American students. In M. J. Tippeconnic Fox, S. C. Lowe, & G. S. McClellan (Eds.), *New directions for student services: Serving Native American students* (no. 109, pp. 33–40). San Francisco: Jossey-Bass.

McInerney, D. M., & Swisher, K. G. (1995). Exploring Navajo motivation in school settings. *Journal of American Indian Education, 34*(3), 28–51.

National Center for Education Statistics (NCES). (2005). *Postsecondary institutions in the United States: Fall 2003 and degrees and other awards conferred: 2002–03.* Washington, DC: U.S. Department of Education.

National Center for Education Statistics (NCES). (2007). *Postsecondary institutions in the United States: Fall 2006 and degrees and other awards conferred: 2005–06.* Washington, DC: U.S. Department of Education.

National Center for Education Statistics (NCES). (2010). *Status and trends in the education of racial and ethnic minorities: 2010–15.* Washington, DC: U.S. Department of Education.

Pascarella, E., & Terenzini, P. T. (1991). *How college affects students: Findings and insights from twenty years of research* (1st ed.). San Francisco: Jossey-Bass.

Pascarella, E., & Terenzini, P. T. (2005). *How college affects students: A third decade of research* (vol. 2). San Francisco: Jossey-Bass.

Pavel, M. D. (1999). American Indians and Alaska Natives in higher education: Promoting access and achievement. In K. G. Swisher (Ed.), *Next steps: Research and practice to advance Indian education* (pp. 239–270). Charleston, WV: ERIC Clearinghouse on Rural Education and Small Schools.

Pavel, M. D., & Padilla, R. V. (1993). American Indian and Alaska Native postsecondary departure: An example of assessing a mainstream model using national longitudinal data. *Journal of American Indian Education, 32*(2), 1–23.

Perry, B. (2002). American Indian victims of campus ethnoviolence. *Journal of American Indian Education, 41*(1), 35–55.

Pewewardy, C., & Frey, B. (2004). American Indian students' perceptions of racial climate, multicultural support services, and ethnic fraud at predominantly White universities. *Journal of American Indian Education, 43*(1), 32–60.

Rai, K. B., & Critzer, J. W. (2000). *Affirmative action and the university: Race, ethnicity, and gender in higher education employment.* Lincoln: University of Nebraska Press.

Reddy, M. A. (1993). *Statistical record of Native North American.* Washington, DC: Gale Research.

Reyhner, J. (1992). American Indians out of school: A review of school-based causes and solutions. *Journal of American Indian Research, 31*(3), 37–56.

Reyhner, J., & Eder, J. (2004). *American Indian education: A history.* Norman: University of Oklahoma Press.

Scott, W. J. (1986). Attachment to Indian culture and the "difficult situation." *Youth and Society, 17*, 381–395.

Shotton, H. J. (2008). *Pathway to the Ph.D.: Experiences of high-achieving American Indian females.* Unpublished doctoral dissertation, University of Oklahoma, Norman.

Shotton, H. J., Oosahwe, E. S. L., & Cintrón, R. (2007). Stories of success: Experiences of American Indian students in a peer-mentoring retention program. *Review of Higher Education, 31*(1), 81–108.

Snyder, T. D., Tan, A. G., & Hoffman, C. M. (2004). *Digest of education statistics 2003.* (NCES 2005-025). Washington, DC: U.S. Department of Education.

Stein, W. J. (2009). Tribal colleges and universities: Supporting the revitalization in Indian country. In L. S. Warner & G. E. Gipp (Eds.), *Tradition and culture in the millennium: Tribal colleges and universities* (pp. 17–34). Charlotte, NC: Information Age.

Swail, W. S., Redd, K. E., & Perna, L. W. (2003). *Retaining minority students in higher education: A framework for success.* ASHE-ERIC Higher Education Report No. 2. Washington, DC: George Washington University, School of Education and Human Development.

Swisher, K., Hoisch, M., & Pavel, D. M. (1991). *American Indian/Alaska Native dropout study*. Washington, DC: National Education Association.

Terenzini, P. T., Pascarella, E. T., & Blimling, G. S. (1996). Students' out-of-class experiences and their influence on cognitive development: A literature review. *Journal of College Student Development, 37*, 149–162

Tierney, W. G. (1990). American Indian higher education in the nineties: A research agenda. Paper presented at the Opening the Montana Pipeline: American Indian Higher Education in the Nineties Conference, Bozeman, MT.

Tierney, W. G. (1992). *Official encouragement, institutional discouragement: Minorities in academe, the Native American experience*. Norwood, NJ: Ablex.

Tinto, V. (1975). Dropout from higher education: A theoretical synthesis of recent research. *Review of Educational Research, 45*, 89–125.

Tinto, V. (1986). Theories of student departure revisited. In J. Smart (Ed.), *Higher education: Handbook of theory and research* (vol. II). New York: Agathon.

Tinto, V. (1993). *Leaving college: Rethinking the causes and cures of student attrition*. Chicago, IL: University of Chicago Press.

Trower, C. A., & Chait, R. P. (2002). Faculty diversity: Too little for too long. *Harvard Magazine, 104*(4), 33–37, 98.

Turner, C. V., González, J. C., & Wood, J. L. (2011). Faculty of color in academe: What 20 years of literature tell us. In S. R. Harper & S. Hurtado (Eds.), *Racial and ethnic diversity in higher education*, ASHE Reader Series (3rd ed., pp. 273–304). Boston: Pearson Learning Solutions.

Waterman, S. J. (2007). A complex path to Haudenosaunee degree completion. *Journal of American Indian Education, 46*(1), 20–40.

Wells, R. N. (1997). *The Native American experience in higher education: Turning around the cycle of failure II*. Canton, NY: St. Lawrence University.

Woodcock, D. B., & Alawiye, O. (2001). The antecedents of failure and emerging hope: American Indians & public higher education. *Education Policy Analysis Archives, 121*, 810–820.

Wright, B. (1985). Programming success: Special student services and the American Indian college student. *Journal of American Indian Education, 24*(1), 1–7.

Wright, B. (1988). For the children of the infidels? American Indian education in the colonial colleges. *American Indian Culture and Research Journal, 12*(3), 1–14.

Wright, B. (1990). American Indian studies programs: Surviving the '80s, thriving in the '90s. *Journal of American Indian Education, 30*(1), 17–24.

I

FIRST-YEAR EXPERIENCE FOR NATIVE AMERICAN FRESHMEN

The University of Arizona First-Year Scholars Program

Amanda Tachine (Diné) and Karen Francis-Begay (Diné)

Sara is Diné from a small community on the Navajo reservation and is the first in her family to attend college. Mixed feelings of excitement and fear surfaced when she first stepped onto the vast and unfamiliar campus of the University of Arizona in Tucson. Raised by her grandmother, she respected her traditional upbringing and personified the Navajo values of humility and hard work. She graduated with honors from high school and was determined to go to college. At freshman orientation, Sara stood among her peers, who appeared to be excited about college, and wondered for a moment if she belonged. Students rushed by her in stylish clothes, some talking on cell phones and all having a sense of confidence. Several of the students and their parents were seeking out resources and asking questions of the orientation staff. Many of the parents were inquisitive and appeared to navigate the college campus with ease.

Sara attended orientation with her mother. Her father, a seasoned construction worker, was not able to attend because he was in another state working to provide for his family. Sara's mom, unfamiliar with the environment, relied on Sara to navigate them through orientation. Sara felt alone and confused going through the orientation experience. Recognizing her daughter's discomfort, Sara's mother asked the orientation staff if there was an office that provided services to Native American students. The staff referred her to the Native American student affairs (NASA) office located centrally on campus. While Sara remained in an orientation meeting, her mother visited NASA and met with and talked to the director, sharing her worries about her daughter coming to a big and unfamiliar university. After this brief visit to NASA and learning more about the programs and services the office provided, she started to feel more positive about Sara's

*chances of surviving at a big university. When she reunited with Sara, she gave
her daughter the director's business card. Immediately Sara took notice of the
director's last name, "Begay," a common Navajo surname. Sara was surprised
but delighted because she was instantly familiar with the name "Begay" and
assumed that the director had ties to the Navajo reservation and was maybe even
clan-related. She commented, "Mom, I think I am going to be fine." Her confidence started to peak once she knew there was a "relative" at a place where she
felt alone.*

This story is true and common for many first-year Native American
students attending college. It illustrates what students like Sara face
when they first arrive on a large, predominantly White college campus. Not all Native American students are the same and they should not be
generalized as having experiences similar to Sara's, but we want to make a
point that Sara's story is real and, unfortunately, often not heard.

This chapter highlights the First-Year Scholars Program (FYSP) at the
University of Arizona (UA), a first-year retention program framed on a
living-learning community model incorporating Native American concepts.
The program has been successful at increasing retention rates of full-time
Native American freshmen from the first to the second year of college and is
considered a "best practices" program. We begin this chapter with an overview of the program's development and essential components, as well as
student perspectives on the program. We conclude with a discussion of challenges facing student support programs for Native American students and
provide recommendations on how to advance the persistence and success of
Native Americans in higher education.

College Access and First-Year Retention Factors

It is important to understand the history of Native American education and
the challenges Native American students face as they prepare for college.
(See the introduction of this book.) The freshman year is a crucial time when
many are overwhelmed and depart college, sometimes for good.

The first year in college is considered the most critical time for all students
(Astin, 1993; Ishler & Upcraft, 2005). Astin's (1993) input-environment-output
model hypothesizes that students enter college with a preestablished set of
characteristics (inputs) that influence their exposure to their environment

(outcomes). Tinto's (1975) interactionalist model of student persistence postulates that academic and social integration influences a student's commitment to the institution and graduation. The more a student is academically and socially integrated into the institution, the higher the rate of persistence. Tierney (1992) challenges Tinto's model of social integration, writing that Native American students are assumed to integrate into the institution. Tierney's position is that rather than students having to integrate, institutions should change to fit the students' cultural needs. Retention models have been largely designed based on mainstream perspectives and lack Native American viewpoints.

A number of factors have been identified as predictors of persistence. The strongest predictor of persistence into the sophomore year is the student's prior academic achievement, including high school grades and scores on college admissions tests (Astin, 1993; Pascarella & Terenzini, 1991). Students with higher socioeconomic status (SES) tend to persist at higher rates than do students from a lower SES (St. John, 1990). Ishler and Upcraft (2005) identified institutional variables, such as selectivity; institutional type (two-year or four-year, private or public); and student variables, such as first-year grade point average and enrollment status (full-time and part-time), as contributors to persistence to the second year.

Many factors affect the persistence of college students, yet many Native American students who enter college encounter a new environment in which differences in values and customs are immediately evident. Having deep-rooted cultural values and strong ties to their tribal communities creates an interdependent value system for Native American students, a contrast to mainstream American society, which prides itself on independence (Huffman, 2008). Markus and Kitayama (1991) refer to the model, *independent view of self,* in which individuals are viewed as autonomous, largely distinct from their relationships, grounded in a variety of features, and interacting with other similarly independent entities. Independent societies mirror aspects of individualistic cultures in which people are more likely to elaborate on independent aspects of themselves that are distinct from others, and to strive to be self-sufficient (Heine, 2008). These values are contrary to most Native American communities, which embody more of an *interdependent view of self* and recognize the importance of connecting with others (Fryberg & Markus, 2007; Markus & Kitayama, 1991). This difference is important to consider when working with Native American students, as they may question their identity and values while in college and when their "way of life" contradicts mainstream values.

Based on family, spirituality, life experiences, and institutional culture, Colbert, Saggio, and Tato (2004) provide strategies for practitioners to increase first-year retention for Native American students. These students are strongly connected to their family and their spirituality and are guided by life experiences. Unfortunately, institutions have fallen short of adapting their services to meet the needs of Native American students. HeavyRunner and Marshall (2003) assert that persistence is derived from self-resilience:

> Resilience is the natural, human capacity to navigate life well. It means coming to know how you think, who you are spiritually, where you come from, and where you are going. It involves understanding our inner spirit and finding a sense of direction. (p. 2)

Self-resilience is a means of persisting in academia because it empowers students to recognize that the "inner spirit" and acknowledging "where you come from" attribute to your success.

The UA and Native American Students

The UA is a public, land-grant, research university in Tucson, Arizona, adjacent to both the Tohono O'odham reservation and Yaqui tribal lands. In 2008 overall enrollment was 37,000 students. The UA continues to have a steady increase in student enrollment, including Native American students. In 2010–2011 the Native American student population reached its highest enrollment—1,153, 3% of the total student body; 225 of these were first-year students. In 2009–2010 the overall first-to-second-year retention rate for all students was 78.1%. The first-to-second-year retention rate for first-time, full-time Native American freshmen ranged from 58.2% in 2006 to 70.9% in 2008, the lowest among other ethnic minority populations (UA Office of Institutional Research & Planning Support, 2010).

Before the FYSP was conceptualized, other student support services and programs existed for Native American students. As illustrated in chapter 5, the UA is rich with unique programs and departments that serve Native Americans. The primary Native American support program on campus is the office of NASA. NASA houses the Wassaja Student Center, which evolved in 1989 after Native American student leaders advocated for a physical space on campus to gather and socialize as a community. Soon after, three other ethnic student support programs were established on campus: Chicano-Hispano Student Affairs (CHSA), African American Student Affairs (AASA), and Asian Pacific American Student Affairs (APASA). The student support programs were originally under the Department of Multicultural Affairs and Student Success (MASS). Over time, there has been a transformation in this department, and the centers currently fall under the dean of students.

History and Impetus for First-Year Scholars Program

In 2003 the director of MASS asked that each center create a first-year "signature" retention program targeting the population it served. NASA already had two unique first-year programs, a residential theme wing in one of the residence halls and a Freshman Composition course for Native American students. The Freshman Composition courses, English 101 and 102, developed in 1990 in partnership with the Department of English, resembled a "learning community" (Smith, MacGregor, Matthews, & Gabelnick, 2004). One section of each composition course, which had seating for 20–25 students, was reserved exclusively for Native American students. These sections incorporated Native American topics on identity, community, history, culture, and language. The course used textbooks and readings on contemporary Native American issues, many authored by Native American scholars. Because the class incorporated a more bicultural curriculum, students were more comfortable and willing to participate in class discussions. As a result, many of these students became better writers and earned better grades.

The second program, known as the "O'odham Ki Wing" (meaning the "Peoples House" in the O'odham language), was created to foster a supportive living community for Native American students. The wing incorporated cultural programming and social activities organized by an upperclass Native American student who served as the hall's resident assistant (RA). The wing's resident headcount grew from 15 students in 2000 to 45 students by 2003.

The Freshman Composition course and the O'odham Ki Wing started out strong, but over time faced some challenges. Although there were efforts to promote the programs to incoming first-year Native American students, participation levels declined. Students and the campus community started to stigmatize the Native American section of the Freshman Composition classes as remedial. A few Native American students who didn't register for the Native American sections expressed more interest in the mainstream

Freshman Composition courses because they did not want to identify as being in a "special" (Native American) section. They noted that their non-Native American peers would tell them that the section was for students who had difficulty adjusting to the UA and the class was "easier" than the other section offerings.

A challenge for the O'odham Ki Wing was its reputation as being a "party wing." Early on, there was little monitoring, supervision, or programming in the wing by the NASA office owing to limited staffing and resources. An effective partnership between NASA and Residence Life was also lacking, and students were not valuing the idea that the wing was focused on creating a healthy and respectful living community for its residents. There needed to be more communication and collaboration between NASA and Residence Life to support the students socially, academically, and culturally. There was also little to no emphasis on programming to promote a healthy and alcohol-/drug-free environment for the wing's residents.

Low participation in the Freshman Composition course and the O'odham Ki Wing also needed to be addressed. It was important to assess whether the programs were having any significant impact on students' making a successful transition to the UA. Early assessments were done but not consistently. It was evident that both programs had positive qualities and, with some restructuring, could be more effective in improving retention. It was determined that changes needed to be made to strengthen the two programs.

First-Year Scholars Program

NASA leadership took action to create a more cohesive and structured program that would integrate both the Freshman Composition course and the O'odham Ki Wing into a learning and living community concept. It was time to bring all components together and develop a holistic model that would provide a supportive community for first-year students. After seeking guidance from the National Resource Center for the First-Year Student Experience and Students in Transition, a clearinghouse for scholarship, policy, and best practice for all postsecondary student transitions, and consulting with campus departments, the FYSP was created. The program emerged as a living-learning community that integrated, reinforced, and strengthened Native American values and traditions into the foundation of the program.

In addition to embedding Native American cultural values, family connect-edness and valuing and promoting a sense of community became key components of the program.

The Learning Community Component

The learning community component of the program is Courses in Common (CIC). Research shows that students who have opportunities to engage with faculty have a higher persistence rate (Tinto, 1993). Therefore, NASA formed relationships with several academic departments to create CIC offerings, which included the Freshman Composition courses for Native American students. Other courses, such as Many Nations of Native America, College Algebra, "Connections" (Freshman Seminar), Chemistry, and a study hall, were added. Each semester, students in the FYSP were required to enroll in the one-unit study hall course, a "Connections" course, and one additional CIC course, which made up half of their full-time semester course load. The study hall and "Connections" course were mandatory in the hopes of being able to monitor the students and do some early intervention work should it be necessary. A NASA staff member was the primary instructor for the study hall course. Students were monitored every week, and referrals were made weekly to academic services, such as tutoring and the Writing Skills Improvement Program, if needed. It was in study hall that the staff usually learned about the nonacademic challenges students were having, such as concerns about financial aid, worrying about an ill family member back home, or not getting along with friends and/or roommates. The study hall was a great way to connect with and support the scholars, as well as allow them to form study groups and support each other.

The Living Community Component

The living community component of the program incorporates the O'odham Ki Wing and includes 30 residential slots for both male and female scholars. Scholars and a Native American RA sign a contract to live in the wing for an entire academic year. After the first year of the program, 10 scholars are invited to return to the wing and serve as mentors to incoming freshmen. Each mentor is expected to work with two to three scholars throughout the year. These students are offered scholarships for their leadership and service as mentors. The wing has grown to house up to 50 scholars, 10 mentors, and two RAs, the largest number of participants to occupy the wing.

One activity that has become an annual cultural tradition for NASA is the blessing of the O'odham Ki Wing. It is a strong belief among many Native Americans that one should bless their living space before they occupy it (see chapter 2). The NASA office invites a community elder or spiritual leader to come to the residence hall to conduct a blessing before the students arrive. The blessing involves prayer and the burning of sweetgrass or sage throughout the living quarters. The blessing is a form of cleansing and is intended to provide protection, safety, and harmony for the residents. Members of the hall staff and other student affairs administrators are invited to participate, and the university administration supports this traditional practice and cooperates with NASA to make the necessary arrangements for the blessing.

Cultural, Social, and Community Activities

Cultural, social, and community engagement among students throughout the year is an integral component of the FYSP. One activity is the FYSP welcome and orientation when students arrive on campus in the early fall and move into the O'odham Ki Wing. A university administrator welcomes the scholars, and parents have an opportunity to meet the NASA staff, CIC faculty, student mentors, and many other campus staff. Parents and family members are given an overview of the FYSP and are encouraged to return to campus for Family Weekend in October when the FYSP plans a special program for family members.

A second fall activity for scholars, mentors, and the NASA staff is a hike to one of the landmarks and scenic destinations in Tucson. During this hike the staff share personal stories about their college experiences and give advice on how to be successful in college. Several icebreakers are conducted so students can open up and get to know one another. A third activity occurs during Family Weekend in October when NASA hosts a barbeque and provides football game tickets to the scholars and their family members. Before NASA organized this family event, few Native American families participated in UA Family Weekend festivities. NASA felt it was important to incorporate parents and family members into campus community events so they, too, could feel a sense of pride and connection to the campus.

In the spring, the scholars engage in a service-learning project with a surrounding Native community. Scholars and their mentors work together to identify a project that will benefit a local tribal community. The service-learning activity provides scholars an opportunity to learn about the local tribal communities and "give back" while also learning how to make valuable connections with the community. A final activity, the highlight of the year, is the end-of-year FYSP celebration. Scholars receive academic recognition from their CIC instructors and get to share highlights of their first-year college experience. Parents, as well as anyone who has had an association with the program, are invited to participate and share in celebrating the scholars' success.

The Professional Team

Another key component of the FYSP is the involvement of a professional team whose members serve in an advisory capacity and help with program improvements. In addition to the NASA and multicultural affairs staff, the professional team is made up of representatives from key departments on campus such as Admissions, Residence Life, Financial Aid, Advising, and the CIC faculty. The professional team interacts with the students and becomes part of the FYSP "family." It provides expertise, advice, and even some comfort to the scholars.

Financial Considerations

A challenge in developing the FYSP was the need for additional resources for staffing and operations. At the inception of the program, the NASA staff consisted of a full-time director, a coordinator, an administrative assistant, and two part-time student workers. The director reconfigured personnel resources to upgrade the coordinator position to assistant director/project manager of the FYSP. After the program's first year, the NASA office was able to secure additional funding through Arizona tribal gaming revenues to meet the added operating costs of the program. Without the additional tribal funding, NASA would have had to dedicate a significant amount of its state budget to the program and severely cut back other programs and services provided to non-FYSP initiatives.

Although there is no cost to students to participate in the program, they are financially responsible for their tuition, course fees, books, and residence hall fees. A majority of the scholars are on financial aid and most are Pell grant–eligible. Many of our faculty, staff, and students volunteer their time in the program, thus limiting the program's overall costs.

Program Strengths

At the conclusion of the FYSP, scholars write end-of-the-year reflection papers that summarize the strengths and weaknesses of the program. Their feedback helps the staff to improve and strengthen the program. Three areas of programmatic strength identified by scholars in these papers are (a) creates a family atmosphere, (b) provides academic support in the CIC, and (c) encourages individual development.

The program prides itself on creating a supportive family atmosphere for scholars. Living in the wing develops a strong connection among scholars, mentors, and RAs. Scholars appreciate the support the RA staff provides and often feel safe and comfortable enough in the wing to leave their doors open, allowing others to enter freely. The wing provides opportunities for lasting friendships to form among students who find they have a lot in common with their peers who are facing similar challenges in coming to college. In addition, the professional team becomes important to these students' navigation and success and they are often referred to as "family."

The CIC component is another strength of the FYSP. Students appreciate having the opportunity to take classes in cohorts with their peers. Having courses with other students who share similar backgrounds instills confidence so that scholars are more willing to actively engage in class. The living-learning design also enables students to form study groups, whether in the residence hall or at the NASA student center. In addition, the "familial" bonds formed with the faculty and graduate assistants who teach the CIC help students to be comfortable getting to know other professors on campus. The relationships the scholars have with the CIC faculty are also beneficial when scholars begin seeking internships or applying to graduate school.

The program encourages scholars to maintain relationships with many who have helped them along the way. As first-year students, this is the first time many of them have been away from home and family. The program provides opportunities for the scholars to grow and be responsible for their success. Many have commented that they are better people as a result of having been in the program. Students recognize that if they had not participated in the program, they might not have lasted at the UA beyond their first year, and they want to see the same success in the cohorts that follow.

Program Challenges

Recent economic cuts to education funding have been extremely difficult for colleges and universities. During times of economic hardship, institutions find ways to continue the vision and mission of their institutions through organizational or transformational change. Institutions are faced with the challenge of organizationally transforming for efficiency and excellence. This often results in significant departmental and programmatic changes, even cuts in staffing and programming.

Budgetary shortfalls have affected the FYSP dramatically, resulting in a reduction in personnel and operations funding that once supported the program. With diminishing resources and staffing, oversight of the program was reassigned to another department, Student Transitions, an area focused on academic retention of undergraduate students. An entirely different staff now manages the program, none of its members are Native American, and the FYSP has evolved into more of a peer-advising program. The FYSP is no longer housed in the NASA office; however, there are mixed expectations that NASA should provide some elements of cultural programming. FYSP activities specific to the living-learning model are no longer are part of the program. Although the name has remained intact, the program has merged with other retention programs that integrate Native American scholars with other students from different ethnic backgrounds. This integration may affect persistence rates, but it is still too soon to know. Having no Native American staff working with the scholars may have implications for the program. No strong connection with NASA will most likely also affect the program. Assessment of whether this organizational change has affected first-to-second-year persistence rates for Native American students has not yet been conducted.

Nationally we are witnessing a growing movement of political initiatives targeting the elimination of programs specifically designed to assist under-represented populations. These political initiatives hamper the growing support and success of programs such as the FYSP. For example, as a result of recent legislation in Arizona, the UA Office of Admissions is not able to do targeted recruitment with preference to race; this affects how Native American students are identified and targeted for programs like the FYSP. More important, these initiatives create a negative perception about the institution's commitment to diversity and are counterproductive to the work that has been done to create an inclusive campus environment. These political challenges create anxiety and frustration, especially when progress has been made to improve access and success for marginalized students who typically do not have the same opportunities as nonmarginalized students.

Recommendations

A key recommendation for developing similar programs that serve Native students is to invest time and effort into understanding student experiences both on and off campus. One way to do this is to invite students to be on committees that focus on enhancing a positive campus climate or address retention challenges. Get to know Native American students early and learn about where they come from and the challenges they are encountering in coming to a big university so that programs can be tailored to address their specific needs.

Administrators should also encourage and support staff and faculty professional development and seek opportunities to gain an awareness and understanding of Native American issues, especially when it comes to educational access and success. This is important for all staff, not just those who are specifically charged with serving Native students. Additionally, staying abreast of Native education issues and scholarship by subscribing to publications like the *Tribal College Journal, Journal of American Indian Education,* or *Winds of Change* magazine can be useful.

A second recommendation is to build relationships with tribes and create advocacy groups to support the recruitment and retention of Native American students. Policy-making decisions are made at the highest levels of administration. It is important to create opportunities for decision makers to visit the tribal communities so they are aware of where their students come from and how difficult the transition from home to college can be. For there to be a paradigm shift in how institutions provide programs and resources for Native American students, the institution's leaders should meet with tribal leaders in their communities. It is also valuable for tribal leaders to visit campus so they can meet with students and provide encouragement and support.

Institutions may also want to involve community members by creating a Native American community advisory group to guide the institution on how it can support its students. This can be particularly useful in helping institutions to understand the economic, social, and educational challenges Native communities face. One example of an advisory group is the UA President's Native American Advisory Council, which is made up of 19 tribal community leaders throughout Arizona. The council meets with the president twice a year to bring forth concerns and to work collaboratively with the administration in improving student recruitment and retention.

Another recommendation is to focus on collaboration and partnerships across campus when developing programs such as the FYSP. Finding ways to collaborate can minimize costs and increase the likelihood that other non-university resources can be identified to support key programs. In addition, strong collaborative and successful programs with multiple invested offices and units are often looked at favorably. Working in isolation is not helpful. Student retention is a campus-wide responsibility, and it is important to engage as many faculty, staff, and departments in this issue as possible. It is even more important to bring student affairs and academic affairs together to work on retention issues.

Conclusion

The first year of college is the most vital time in any student's higher education experience. For Native American students, we contend that it is significantly more crucial to have a successful and positive first-year experience that will be the foundation for the remaining years of their college experiences. The FYSP is a great example of how institutions can provide such a foundation. The program operates from a holistic framework, creating a family atmosphere, nourishing relationships with academic and student affairs departments, and understanding and respecting the Native American students, their families, and their home communities. As our society shifts through economic downturns, maneuvers through institutional and organizational changes, and faces many political agendas, strong advocacy to maintain programs like the FYSP is important if we are to gain an advantage in the retention landscape.

We want students like Sara to succeed in college. Her story is real and should be heard, because she is an important thread in the weaving of that tapestry of success. Sara's story ends on a positive note. She persisted through her undergraduate education and graduated at the top of her class. During her undergraduate career, she held many leadership positions and studied abroad. She plans to eventually attend law school. Sara credits the FYSP for her success and always shares that message with college-bound students.

References

Astin, A. (1993). What matters in college. *Liberal Education, 79*(4), 4–15.

Colbert, C. R., Saggio, J. J., & Tato, D. (2004). Transforming the first-year experience for American Indians/Alaska Natives. In L. I. Rendón, M. Garcia, & D. Person (Eds.), *Transforming the first year of college for students of color* (pp. 137–160). Columbia: National Resource Center for the First-Year Experience & Students in Transition, University of South Carolina.

Fryberg, S., & Markus, H. (2007). Cultural models of education in American Indian, Asian American and European American contexts. *Social Psychology of Education, 10*, 213–246.

HeavyRunner, I., & Marshall, K. (2003). Miracle survivors: Promoting resilience in Indian students. *Tribal College, 14*(4). Retrieved August 6, 2011, from, http://proquest.umi.com.ezp.lib.rochester.edu/pqdwebdid = 495904591&sid = 2&Fmt = 3&clientId = 17941&RQT = 309&VName = PQD

Heine, S. J. (2008). *Cultural psychology.* New York: W.W. Norton.

Huffman, T. (2008). *American Indian higher education experiences: Cultural visions and personal journeys.* New York: Peter Lang.

Ishler, J. L., & Upcraft, M. L. (2005). The keys to first-year student persistence. In M. L. Upcraft, J. N. Gardner, & B. O. Barefoot (Eds.). *Challenging and supporting the first-year student* (pp. 27–46). San Francisco: Jossey-Bass.

Markus, H. R., & Kitayama, S. (1991). Culture and self: Implications for cognition, emotion, and motivation. *Psychology Review, 98,* 224–253.

Pascarella, E., & Terenzini, P. T. (1991). *How college affects students: Findings and insights from twenty years of research* (1st ed.). San Francisco: Jossey-Bass.

Smith, B. L., MacGregor, J., Matthews, R., & Gabelnick, F. (2004). *Learning communities: Reforming undergraduate education.* San Francisco: Jossey-Bass.

St. John, E. P. (1990). Price response in persistence decisions: An analysis of the high school and beyond senior cohort. *Research in Higher Education, 31*(4), 387–403.

Tierney, W. (1992). An anthropological analysis of student participation in college. *Journal of Higher Education, 63*(6), 603–618.

Tinto, V. (1975). Dropout from higher education: A theoretical synthesis of research. *Review of educational research, 45*(1), 89–125.

Tinto, V. (1993). *Leaving college: Rethinking the causes and cures of student attrition* (2nd ed.). Chicago: University of Chicago Press.

University of Arizona (UA) Office of Institutional Research & Planning Support. (2010). Retrieved November 10, 2011, from http://factbook.arizona.edu

2

INCORPORATING NATIVE CULTURE INTO STUDENT AFFAIRS

Steven C. Martin (Muscogee Creek) and
Adrienne L. Thunder (Ho-Chunk)

For Grandma and Grandpa, Jean Galey, Velva Lu.
—Steve

Growing up, my Native culture was defined by burning cedar in a Folgers' coffee can, wild onions, Fourth Sunday church services, and writing Creek words in my Big Chief notebook as grandma explained their meaning. It meant listening to older ones share stories in our Creek language at Uncle Hixie's farm, being told by Grandma Polly that eating a Grand Daddy Longlegs heals skin boils, and Grandma Florence frying me an egg each time I visited, no matter what time of day. Culture meant grieving properly for our loved ones as we laid them to rest. This is what I know.

I was told by my grandpa that he was once asked to record our Creek hymns on tape. He was told these tapes would be sold and shared by many. Grandpa guessed the "many" meant White people. Grandpa declined the offer because, as he put it to me, "I cannot give them something they will not understand." He knew our songs, our prayers, and our language held our spirit, and no English words could really translate them.

These cultural experiences have helped formulate my cultural understanding, and they influence what I share and with whom I share. During the process of writing this chapter, Adrienne and I discussed our connections with our own tribal ways and how we have been affected by our educational journeys. We talked about times we felt lost and misunderstood, and acknowledged people who gave us guidance and encouragement to help us find our way. We write this chapter to honor our grandparents, relatives, elders and older ones, and many others we were blessed to have in our lives to offer us guidance and knowledge. We hope to help student affairs practitioners develop an appreciation for and a way to work with our Native peoples. Most important, we write this chapter to honor our Native American college students.

For my grandparents, Dads, Cuwis, Moms, Tegas, siblings, and especially my children.
—Adrienne

Upon graduating from high school, and again after graduating from college, my parents sponsored Native American Church services for me. I grew up in that church, hearing songs, prayers, and lessons in life in English and in Ho-Chunk, learning who I am, what my people stood for, and what they hoped for me in my education. As I grew up I was advised not to go too far away from the light of the fireplace. It was something I heard my elders tell many young people who were about to leave home to embark upon their educational or professional pursuits. What it meant to me was to not forget who I am, to care for my spirit, not to forget the humble people I come from, and not to forget all the good teachings I was fortunate enough to have received while I was growing up.

Our teachings have carried Ho-Chunk people far; our oral history tells us we have been through two Ice Ages and at least five removals from our homelands. As I think about and observe the Ho-Chunk youth today, I consider my life's experiences with Ho-Chunk culture and the precious little I know. I understand better now the worries my elders and ancestors had for our people and for our way of life.

These concerns are not new. Since Indian people began participating in Euro-American education, we have deliberated retaining our tribal identities and traditions as we considered our futures (Patterson, 2002). After over a century, educated Indian people are still contemplating some of the same issues they were back then. It is good to know we still have some choice in the matter. We continue to bear the responsibility to keep our cultural knowledge and traditions a part of our educational experiences and our students' experiences as we look toward our shared future.

Culture, to me, is to live with compassion and love for one another, to share what we have, to help one another, to live a balanced life, and to be thankful for what the Creator has given us. There are rules, protocols, and procedures for almost everything, including how to conduct myself and how to express myself. I grew up knowing everything had a place and that, most important, I had a place—in my family, in my clan, in my tribe, and in the world. I learned from what my elders taught me, that I am important. I am needed, as we all are needed, to uphold my place and my responsibilities within each set of relationships.

This chapter begins with why we believe cultural programming is important, and continues by informing the reader of the importance of elders, traditional knowledge, and ceremony in our communities. What *culture* means in and among Indigenous communities varies greatly, and incorporating culture into student affairs requires great care and consideration. Our intention here is to highlight ways in which institutions may honor what specific Native communities and individuals may bring to their campus. We discuss aspects of Native culture to promote validation and inclusion. We then introduce a culturally relevant model for Native students, the Sacred Hoop. We conclude with recommendations for practice and, as we began, with personal reflection.

During our careers in higher education, as students and as professionals, we have witnessed Native students demonstrate incredible determination to achieve success. Their resilience is inspired, in part, by the survival and accomplishments of numerous tribal generations. Student organizations, services, and programs exist to aid the development of students at most non-Native colleges and universities (NNCUs). Based on our experiences, and those described in the literature (Brayboy, 2004; Garrod & Larimore, 1997; Jackson, Smith, & Hill, 2003; Lowe, 2005; Waterman, 2007), these efforts are not always sensitive to the cultural needs of Native students. We believe Native cultures should be incorporated into student affairs practice because our students' strength and resilience is rooted in a healthy, balanced sense of self. We think about Native American students who, like us, enter college with a record of accomplishment and the love, support, and prayers of their families, and those students who use college as an antidote to the destructiveness of home, with only the hope that education will help heal their spirits.

Incorporating culture in student affairs can also provide a needed buffer against the exclusionary messages Native students receive. At times, these messages assault their very personhood. NNCUs have their own cultural language, symbols, traditions, rituals, and protocols for which they are known, and these are held as the ideal. To participate in an institution's traditions means holding these same symbols, traditions, or rituals in high regard. These ideals often exclude Native Americans or, worse, glorify a past that champions our subjugation and dispossession. Mascots are an obvious example, but other subtle and ubiquitous instances also exist. Many U.S. colleges uphold Western civilization as the educational and institutional ideal. Cultural discontinuity or inconsistency between the student's home culture and that of the institution arises as Native students feel a conflict in perspectives and values (Waterman, 2007), leading them to question their degree of belonging at such an institution. We renew the call by Garrod and Larimore (1997) for a student development paradigm shift to culturally relevant approaches and models to serve our students.

Incorporating Native culture in student affairs is important and necessary because as our students continue to experiment, grow, and learn, they must have the capacity to carry with them what is most essential, their cultural identity. To have the elements needed for their continued growth, a familiar context with rules for participation that Native students recognize and understand, including a sense that they are important, valued members of their campus community, is also necessary. For many traditional Native people, education "historically occurred in a holistic social context that developed a sense of importance of each individual as a contributing member of the social group" (Cajete, 2005, p. 69). Campuses that incorporate Native culture into their student affairs policies and practices provide a way for students to interact with the campus in positive ways.

Incorporating Native Culture Into Student Affairs

There is no formula, nor any one model, that will effortlessly lead to effective programming for Native students. The 4Rs approach (Kirkness & Barnhardt, 1991), however, is one NNCUs should consider, not only in student affairs, but in all aspects of institutional operation. Adhering to the four principles of respect, relevance, reciprocity, and responsibility can assist Natives and non-Natives alike in creating a better understanding of differences. Incorporating the 4Rs and drawing on local tribal resources can help alleviate Native students' feelings of isolation and marginalization, or worse, assault on and devaluation of their cultural ways. Using this approach, student affairs practitioners can design programs and services to meet the needs unique to Native students.

Some student affairs and academic affairs staff, faculty members, and Native students have brought ways of incorporating Native culture into both programming and pedagogy. There have been successful efforts to make institutions more hospitable and relevant to Native students and to create opportunities for non-Native students, faculty, and staff to learn about Native peoples. Campuses need more quality programs to dispel myths and to show us as modern people confronting substantive modern issues.

Culture-based programs help to provide authentic, contemporary representations of Native people. Programs and events offered from this perspective can be beneficial for all who participate. These events and programs can allow all students and university personnel to take part in the Native community in ways that fit and enrich their already-busy lives in fun, educational, and inclusive ways. Finally, they offer opportunities for the campus Native community and local Native community to maintain ties and develop mutual support.

To establish a stronger connection with Native students, student affairs practitioners need to expand their tribal knowledge of the students and communities they serve. Doing so demonstrates a commitment to Native students and provides better perspective for their stories. Tribal communities contain a wealth of knowledge, and visits to them are demonstrations of respect and should be undertaken as such. Awareness of the history of the land on which the university is built can also be very important because it may be culturally significant to the tribes in the area or region. For example, the University of Idaho sits on the Palouse, a sacred gathering place for the Nez Perce people (Slickpoo & Walker, 1973). The University of Wisconsin–Madison campus contains burial and effigy mounds (University of Wisconsin, 2008) connected to tribes from the region, including the Ho-Chunk. This simple recognition of a truth significant to local tribal people can have multiple positive outcomes.

In traditional tribal communities, elder knowledge is highly valued, particularly language instruction and spiritual guidance, and universities can benefit from including this knowledge in cultural programming. Student affairs programs that involve elders can bring a greater sense of comfort, connection, and belonging among Native American students; and strengthen bonds among the university, Native American students, and tribal communities.

We believe cultural events and ceremonies can have the power to heal or reenergize one's spirit. As more attention is being paid to all students' spiritual development in student affairs (Palmer, 1999; Parks, 2000), we note the one need most underdeveloped for our students, their spirituality. For Native students who place high value on their spirituality, this can be an especially difficult part of their lives to put on hold or find alternate ways to practice until they return home. Unlike larger faith systems and affiliations (e.g., Christian, Jewish, or Islamic faiths, etc.), traditional Native spiritual practices are unique to each tribe and are often place-based. There are no churches, synagogues, or mosques for our practices and, therefore, no easily accessible way for students to practice their traditional spirituality on campus. There is no substitute for these tribally specific, community-based ceremonies. Institutions can, however, help facilitate a process to help students meet some of their spiritual needs.

Smudging, for example, is a purification ceremony that involves burning sage, sweetgrass, or cedar to cleanse a person or a place. Before students get settled in their residence halls, some will want to smudge their rooms, making their new "homes" spiritually clean. Universities generally have policies prohibiting the burning of materials inside facilities, but this prohibition can be amended. The University of Montana and the University of Wisconsin–Stevens Point are two campuses that have implemented smudging policies allowing students to conduct this ceremony. The University of Montana policy allows for "smudging associated with cultural rituals consistent with traditional ceremonies and observances. Smudging may incorporate the smoke of sage, sweet grass, cedar, and other related medicinal plants as elements of purification and sacred ceremony" (University of Montana, 2009). Smudging is restricted to designated spaces, signs are posted, and in most cases university officials are notified before the ceremony. Although still not ideal, this type of policy demonstrates an important first step institutions can take to assist Native students in meeting their unique needs.

Cultural programming should be more than pow-wows and events limited to Native American Heritage Month. That being said, pow-wows are popular on university campuses (though not all tribal people pow-wow); however, the responsibility for coordinating a pow-wow typically rests on the shoulders of a few Native students and the Native student organization. Planning and implementing such a large event can be overwhelming for students, and their grades are often affected by this burden. Therefore, devoting staff to coordinate these (and other) large events is needed. As student affairs professionals know, it is important for those responsible for planning programs or events to consider program goals and objectives, participants, and context. We see Native students' engagement in such programming to be crucial as acts of survivance (Vizenor, 1994, in Brayboy, 2004). For Native students to continue the stories and traditions of their own peoples, as well as their personal, academic, and career development, these students must not only be allowed, but actively encouraged, to incorporate their stories and traditions into their ongoing learning processes.

Culturally Relevant Model: The Sacred Hoop

We contend that creating and implementing culturally relevant and developmental models and programs is essential for the full involvement and participation of Native Americans. One example is the Sacred Hoop Model, co-created by Scott Zlotak and Steven Martin out of respect for underserved Lakota, Dakota, and Nakota (L/D/N) college students in South Dakota. Scott and Steve were honored and humbled to be entrusted by the L/D/N communities with this knowledge to help their people, and the Sacred Hoop Model became an exercise of their shared responsibility for the well-being of their students. The model provides a culture-based approach to support the development of Native American students as they navigate through higher education. Proper cultural protocol requires us to give respectful tribute to those L/D/N spiritual leaders, here in this world and in the spirit world, who shared the sacred knowledge and granted their approval to the creation of this model. Sacred knowledge is regarded with respect and appreciation among tribal people, and we ask readers to keep this teaching in mind as they begin to understand this model.

The Sacred Hoop Model is based on L/D/N ceremonial philosophies. The process of the Sacred Hoop Model is the same four-phase process found in the L/D/N *Inipi* (Sweat Lodge) ceremony: Calling, Welcoming, Healing (Processing), and Releasing. Using concepts of the Sacred Hoop, student programs and services can be created to better represent and acknowledge the active participation of American Indian students in institutions of higher education. Occurring before students arrive on campus, the Calling process includes extensive, sensitively conducted recruitment and outreach. During this phase, university representatives make efforts to "call" out to prospective Native American students. If recruitment is conducted with integrity, involves extended families, and emphasizes respect, first-year students will establish an early, essential connection with the university and have some mental preparation on the fundamentals (i.e., student organizations, support services and programs) needed to survive in college.

The Welcoming phase marks student transition throughout the first year and into the second year at the university. Transition programs and academic enhancement classes provide a developmentally enriched environment. Through appropriate services that acknowledge the gifts Native students bring and provide support as needed, students develop a greater bond with the institution and feel genuinely "welcomed." Advisors can encourage greater involvement in cocurricular and academically related activities by students, strengthening their growing connections with the school and drawing on individual student interests and abilities. New student orientation programs, potlucks and socials, and multicultural clubs can all be key tools for building connections for Native students who need to know who their allies and friends are, and who to approach with questions or concerns. Many (but not all) of these people will be Native faculty and staff members. Though the term *helicopter parents* is used to describe parents who are overly involved with their child's or children's experiences in higher education (Cline & Fay, 1990), this label and concept are inappropriate to apply to Native American parents or families. It is a cultural value and responsibility of Native relatives to be highly involved in their children's lives. Culturally aware student affairs staff members may struggle with this in the age of the Family Educational Rights and Privacy Act (FERPA), the Health Insurance Portability and Accountability Act (HIPAA), and similar legal restrictions, but they still need to find acceptable ways of helping students and the institution communicate with Native families.

In the third phase, students start evaluating or "Processing" their current status and begin to prepare properly for the next transition. Universities encourage upperclass students to declare majors and to accept more leadership roles and responsibilities. Students begin to engage in professional preparation programs and plan for graduation. Student organizations, student government, and ambassador programs are platforms all students use to establish themselves as leaders. Many campuses have created peer-mentoring programs, which allow students to give back, connecting with a core value of most Native cultures. Sharing or giving responsibility shows respect and trust, enhancing student leadership qualities and strengthening a bond with the university. An important strategy in the processing phase is to continue to include relatives and tribal members. Feedback from these key constituency groups is valuable to students' decision-making processes. Tribal communities can help students by connecting with those who desire to give back and helping others find grants, internships, part-time or summer work, or graduate school leads, which are essential to success in the Processing phase.

In the final stage, Releasing, graduating students are "released" to take on new endeavors. We have seen many Native students experience difficulties during this change as they consider graduate school, work, and serving their communities. Student affairs professionals will want to build relationships with campus departments, such as career planning and placement, to connect students with internships or professional training activities. Career fairs and service-learning programs also help contribute to proper preparation for life after graduation. Student affairs practitioners must expand their strategies to include cultural leadership models, particularly those influenced by Native American leadership methods. These models support the goals of fostering an engaged tribal citizenry, upholding tribal sovereignty, and meeting tribal community needs and students' career development goals (Johnson, 1997, in Benham & Stein, 2003). One other important approach is to expose students to strong Native American role models. All phases are important in the Sacred Hoop Model, but special attention must be given to this final phase for smooth transition to occur. Proper implementation of the Sacred Hoop Model allows for the full expression and involvement of Native Americans in institutions of higher learning. The cultural imprint of the model creates balance between "new" knowledge and cultural wisdom.

Recommendations

As with any other population of students, there is no secret to, nor one way of, working with Native students. Given this country's long and largely adversarial history with regard to Native Americans and how each tribal nation experienced European contact and its aftermath, we hope student affairs practitioners realize why Native students might be reluctant to trust and respect non-Native professionals and institutions. Remembering their context is a necessary start to connecting with Native students. We offer the following recommendations with that goal in mind:

- Be authentic. Be humble and sincere. Be patient, as it may take more time to build a trusting relationship with some Native students. Reluctant Native students will eventually come to trust that you have their best interests at heart. Learn to laugh at yourself. Native students, like most other students, are attracted to good humor.
- Be a teacher and a student; do not be afraid to learn. Listen to and encourage students to establish what they would like to achieve; help them work toward their goals with the expectation that they will succeed. This approach puts students in charge of their own experiences, while student affairs staff follow their lead. It also requires both students and staff to be accountable for carrying out their respective responsibilities to make success possible.
- Mentoring programs must provide students with encouragement and support that takes into account each student and his or her cultural

orientation. A well-supported mentor program provides training on how to address common questions, access resources, solve problems, and develop personalized strategies for academic and personal success.

- Work toward helping your institution become more accommodating to students' spiritual developmental needs. Since Native students already feel they are the subject of surveillance (Brayboy, 2004), they are likely to keep their spiritual practices private. This raises two points: first, students need a place to practice their tribal spiritual traditions with as little interference as possible. Second, student affairs staff may need to offer a general invitation to students to ask for whatever accommodations they may need in this regard. This must be done with respect for student privacy. We have presented examples of university policies that were enacted to accommodate smudging, as one example, but other areas require this same type of accommodation.

- Indigenous students (and faculty and staff) need their own cultural space on campus. If an institution does not have a Native American student or cultural center, it should do what it can to provide such a space so it can accommodate specific needs such as those listed in these recommendations. Having such a space demonstrates care for and commitment to the campus Native community.

- Depending on the size of the institution, having more than one staff person to serve in Native American student affairs, at least one male and one female, would be ideal. On many campuses, a sole staff position is responsible for supporting Native students. Our recommended configuration better allows for both staff members to do their day-to-day work while also finding the time to develop and maintain relationships inherent to the health of a campus Native community. Further, in some tribal traditions, there are some tasks that typically women do for other women (e.g., handling certain ceremonial matters but also issues surrounding pregnancy, children, and families) and others that men typically do for other men (e.g., handling certain ceremonial matters, being a drum keeper).

- Involve Native faculty and staff in programming and events. There are often competing demands for faculty members' and fellow staff members' time, but these key people have the potential to provide students with important opportunities for their cognitive, professional, and personal development. A sustained effort to include them is well worth it. Since they may feel like "the only one" in their respective departments, including them and helping them get to know the students will be helpful to them as well.

- Remember that extended families are important to Native student success. When possible, develop cultural programming and events that include families, much like the Family Education Model (Heavy-Runner & DeCelles, 2002) suggests. On larger campuses, this will be challenging, but if key personnel (e.g., Native faculty, staff, administrators) are involved, and contact between those involved occurs regularly and in a meaningful way, family programs could be very successful.
- Use the 4Rs of respect, relevance, reciprocity, and responsibility in your work with Native students (Kirkness & Barnhardt, 1991). As an advisor, residence hall director, student activities coordinator, or dean of students—whatever your role with Native American students—this approach will be highly useful.

Further, consider creating your own culturally based model of student affairs practice. The Sacred Hoop Model is an example based on concepts from the L/D/N tribal peoples. What are the core values or key practices of Native people in your area on which you might draw? How can you involve tribal elders with your Native students in developing new, unique ways of conceptualizing student development at your institution?

Conclusion

This chapter focused on the importance of incorporating culture into programming for Native American students. We shared our personal and professional experiences and introduced the Sacred Hoop Model. We began this chapter with our understanding of culture, and we end the chapter with our understanding of the intersection of culture and education.

Adrienne:

I was not yet seven years old when I first stepped onto a college campus. My Cuwis (aunts) brought me there on occasion while they attended college, and as I was growing up, they helped me to get there. From them, I learned this was a worthy endeavor, and I would take what I learned and use it to help my people or other Indian people someday.

When I look at the efforts Indigenous people undertake to restore or maintain their nations—spiritually, culturally, politically, economically—I am humbled and inspired to learn more so I may do more. Indigenous people face the same challenges other communities face in a poor economy with an unfavorable political climate. Higher education can be a part of our efforts to keep our tribal nations strong. In order for that to happen, colleges and universities must be willing and able to accommodate the various cultural perspectives our Indigenous young people bring to higher education. More important, our young people must feel that they have a place there and that they are important and needed, because they are.

Steve:

My Grandma and Grandpa never sat me down and said, "This is culture" or "This is what it means to be Indian." When I attended college people tried to tell me what culture was, and how to be Indian. And since I did not meet their standards, I was often alienated—set apart from my peers and set apart from my own identity. No Native college student should be asked to check his or her cultural identity at the college gate. Fortunately, over time, I was able to find support from trustworthy staff and peers who impacted my commitment to success, and they continue to inspire me today.

During my time as a professional in higher education, I have frequently questioned whether I am serving a helpful purpose or providing an injustice to our young Native students by helping them stay in an environment that does not understand them. Ironically, my academic, professional, and, most important, my life's accomplishments are attributed to my experiences in higher education. As Native peoples, we honor the value of generosity—of giving back. It would be a disservice now, if I didn't give back to Native American college students all that has been given me. It is my cultural obligation to ensure that the stories of Native students be respected and to inspire confidence in the expression of their cultural identities. The diverse stories of our Native students can only enrich a college campus.

My grandpa was a good man, and I know he is proud of what I am doing. His spirit is always with me, and I can hear him saying, "You are doing good, cēpvnē."

References

Benham, M. K. P. A, & Stein, W. J. (Eds.). (2003). *The renaissance of American Indian higher education: Capturing the dream*. Mahwah, NJ: Lawrence Erlbaum.

Brayboy, B. M. J. (2004). Hiding in the ivy: American Indian students and visibility in elite educational settings. *Harvard Educational Review, 74*(2), 125–152.

Cajete, G. (2005). American Indian epistemologies. In M. J. T. Fox, S. C. Lowe, & G. S. McClennan, (Eds.), Serving Native American students, *New Directions for Student Services* (no. 109, pp. 69–78). San Francisco: Jossey-Bass.

Cline, F. W., & Fay, J. (1990). *Parenting with love and logic: Teaching children responsibility.* Colorado Springs, CO: NavPress.

Garrod, A., & Larimore, C. (Eds.). (1997). *First person, first peoples: Native American college graduates tell their life stories.* Ithaca, NY: Cornell University Press.

HeavyRunner, I., & DeCelles, R. (2002). Family education model: Meeting the student retention challenge. *Journal of American Indian Education, 41*(2), 29–37.

Jackson, A. P., Smith, S. A., & Hill, C. L. (2003). Academic persistence among Native American college students. *Journal of College Student Development, 44*(4), 548–565.

Kirkness, V. J., & Barnhardt, R. (1991). First Nations and higher education: The four Rs—respect, relevance, reciprocity, responsibility. *Journal of American Indian Education, 30*(3), 1–15.

Lowe, S. C. (2005). This is who I am: Experiences of Native American students. In M. J. T. Fox, S. C. Lowe, & G. S. McClennan (Eds.) Serving Native American students, *New Directions for Student Services* (no. 109, pp. 33–40). San Francisco: Jossey-Bass.

Palmer, P. (1999). *Let your life speak: Listening for the voice of vocation.* San Francisco: Jossey-Bass.

Parks, S. D. (2000). *Big questions, worthy dreams: Mentoring young adults in their search for meaning, purpose, and faith.* San Francisco: Jossey-Bass.

Patterson, M. W. (2002). "Real" Indian songs. *American Indian Quarterly, 26*(1), 44–66.

Slickpoo, A. P., Jr., & Walker, D. E., Jr. (1973). Treaty with the Nez Perces, 1855, Art. 2, in *Noon nee-me-poo (We, the Nez Perces): Culture and history of the Nez Perces* (vol. 1, p. 286). Lapwai, ID: Nez Perce Tribe of Idaho.

University of Montana. (2009, May). Smudging policy. Policy Number: 201.5. American Indian Student Services website. Retrieved from http://life.umt.edu/aiss/Smudging%20Policy.php

University of Wisconsin. (2008, November). Ancient mounds make UW-Madison a unique landscape. Retrieved from http://www.news.wisc.edu/15910

Waterman, S. J. (2007). A complex path to Haudenosaunee degree completion. *Journal of American Indian Education, 46*(1), 20–40.

3

EXTENDING THE RAFTERS

Cultural Context for Native American Students

Dr. Timothy Ecklund and Danielle Terrance (Mohawk)

T he Haudenosaunee (also known as the Iroquois) are the people of the longhouse. The longhouse was a large, extended home for the extended clan family that also served as a place for meetings and ceremonies. Because the Haudenosaunee are a matrilineal society, when a man and woman married, the man moved into the longhouse of his wife. In Haudenosaunee culture, there is a concept of "extending the rafters," which is literally expanding the longhouse to make room for new families. Creating Native American program houses and/or living-learning units to represent a kind of multifamily home has the double purpose of providing a residential unit and a cultural center. Like the concept of a longhouse, these units can reinforce Native American values and provide a safe space. College campuses can extend their Native culture rafters in culturally appropriate and respectful ways through the creation of Native American living-learning units.

Deloria and Wildcat (2001) describe Native American identity as a combination of power and place. *Power* is defined as "being the living energy that inhabits and/or composes the universe" (p. 22–23), while *place* is described as "being the relationship of things to each other" (p. 23). Important to understanding these concepts is the insight that Indigenous people view the world in the particular. Deloria explains that the particular refers to a real time-specific understanding of one's environment and the interconnectedness of its inhabitants. Through this knowledge it is possible to incorporate more complete information when making decisions. It is a personal relationship that does not expand to encompass a universal truth. It would therefore follow that knowing one's place in the universe begins by knowing one's place in the most immediate community, and this is where life's energy is derived. Deloria and Wildcat (2001) assert that power and place produce personality, and that we have a personal and moral relationship with the universe.

The purpose of this chapter is to share our experience with Native American–themed living units. We begin with an explanation of the importance of place for Native Americans, why we think it is important to have these units, and institutional organizational structures. Then we discuss Akwe:kon at Cornell University and Jakonsase House at the State University of New York at Buffalo as examples. Next, we discuss working with the campus, challenges, and finally, recommendations.

The Importance of Defining Place Within the Campus Context for Native Americans

It has been well documented that Native American students who start college at non-Native colleges and universities (NNCUs) often find it difficult to connect with the institution as they face a cultural divide that acts as a barrier to their success (Ecklund, 2005; Tierney 1992). Lowe (2005) describes how she struggled during the first year of college despite the fact that she was academically well prepared, had received scholarships and other financial incentives, moved into a campus residence hall, and seemed to have everything going for her. Such stories are repeated over and over again at numerous institutions across our country where Native American students are found (Garrod & Larimore, 1997). For many of these students, the cultural conflicts they encounter on college campuses can be overwhelming, disempowering, and, in some cases, completely debilitating.

Living on campus is a challenging adjustment for which many college students are not prepared (Barefoot, 2008). For Native American students, the transition to residence hall living may be more complicated and difficult. How connected or immersed students are in their Native American culture may have a significant impact on their transition to residence hall living. Community is a very important part of the Native American culture. The place where a Native American college student lives is an essential component of his or her success at the institution. For Native American students whose home is not near the college, living on campus may be their only choice. With this in mind, offering culturally relevant spaces and programs becomes an essential component of Native American student success and can make a world of difference in how these students navigate their daily existence.

Imagine if there were a place on your campus for Native American students to live with other Native American students, a place that explicitly values Native American traditions and culture. This could be a place where Native American images were present and culturally important times of the year were understood and celebrated. And, most important, this could be a place where Native American students could come "home" at the end of a long day of classes and feel like they belong. To help Native American students survive and thrive at NNCUs, culturally relevant living units have been introduced at some institutions. Cornell University and Dartmouth College have experienced great success with these units.

Programmatic Themed Living and Learning Communities/ Cultural Floors

Today, campus living options such as first-year student halls, fully furnished apartments, drug- and alcohol-free areas, wellness centers, fraternity or sorority houses, and so on, are available at most institutions. Colleges and universities have come to realize that one traditional-style "dormitory" does not fit all students, and that there is great educational potential for constructing value-added living experiences in the form of living-learning programs (LLPs) (Zeller, 2008).

During the 1970s and 1980s, many NNCUs developed cultural centers in residence halls as living-learning programs to support and celebrate primarily the African or African American cultural experience (Patton, 2005). These centers were intended to infuse a constant presence of African American culture into the campus while also providing a place for African American students to live together, along with White students who shared an interest in African American culture (Patton, 2005). As college and university populations diversified, these offerings were expanded at some institutions to accommodate Latino/Latina and Asian students (Hurtado, Milem, Clayton-Pederson, & Allen, 1996; Min Liu, Cuyjet, & Lee, 2010). Not so frequently found were similar programs for Native American students (Garrod & Larimore, 1997). As academic programs for Native American students emerged, living-learning options were also introduced.

Within the broad array of living-learning programs are culturally themed living areas. Although similar to other living-learning initiatives, culturally themed living areas have several distinct purposes (Hurtado et al., 1996; Patton, 2005). Foremost among these is the opportunity to bring students of a particular cultural background into a living environment that directly supports them and their culture. The introduction of these types of living-learning programs not only brings attention to the challenges many students of color face, but also enlivens interest in the cultures these students represent. For some students, residing in a culturally themed living program allows them to explore their cultural identity, which is an important part of the student development process.

Why Special Living Units for Native Students?

Native students are not the only students who face academic or social issues in the transition to college, but they do have the lowest enrollment rate in higher education institutions and the lowest graduation rates in comparison to other ethnic groups (Jackson, Smith, & Hill, 2003; Snyder, Tan, & Hoffman, 2006). Researchers have found that students who participated in LLPs reported smoother academic and social transitions to college and viewed the residence hall environment as more supportive of their academic and social lives (Johnson et al., 2007). In addition to these findings, students who participated in LLPs reported having spent more time discussing academic topics and having more frequent interaction with faculty (Inkelas, Szelényi, Soldner, & Brower, 2007). Finally, students reported more confidence in their academic skills and a greater likelihood of graduating from college (Inkelas, Soldner, & Szelényi, 2008).

Research on the experiences of Native American living units is limited. The following observations are from students who have lived in Native American living units at universities in New York State.

> It was during my first semester that I realized how rare a species Native American/Haudenosaunee students are in a college environment. I thought this would make me feel isolated in classrooms full of non-Native students who are coming from a different background than myself. I think this is where the Native American Suite really helped me maintain my sense of personal and cultural identity as a Native American, specifically Haudenosaunee, student. Having a support network of other Native students around taught me that I wasn't alone in my educational pursuits and

unique trials of difficulty. Because, at the time I entered, I was the only freshman Native American student, the other students really became both mentors and friends to me—they showed me around campus, advised me which faculty teach the best classes, showed me how to navigate the headache-inducing financial aid and registration problems that often arose for me, and also became lifelong friends that I still visit with and keep in touch with often. When I reflect back to my years in college, I am certain that the suite has attributed to my success in that environment and beyond into my achievements today. —Shannon (Tuscarora)

The suite gave me a better understanding of who I truly was and it helped me better understand myself from a Native American cultural standpoint. Living with the other Native American students, who came from various tribes and clans, taught me unity, respect for all, and most of all, friendship. Now, more than ever, I am proud to say I am a Native American student, and I played a part in the growth and understanding of my people on the campus. —Ron (Seneca)

As these narratives indicate, it becomes apparent that, for these students, living together and sharing in their common culture were contributors to their persistence and graduation. As noted in the introduction to this book, HeavyRunner and DeCelles's (2002) Family Education Model identifies the connection to families as an essential component of student success. As these quotes illustrate, Native American living units are positioned to include families in two important ways. If a student is far from home, the living unit becomes a source of extended family support as students learn to rely on each other. These areas also become important places to practice ceremonies and create traditional expressions. For students who live near the campus, the residential program becomes a place to host family members and introduce them to the university. Two sisters who attended a university with a living area for Native American students would have never been allowed by their parents to live on campus had it not been for the Native American living unit. The authors were informed that once the family visited the program, they were assured it would be a supportive place for their daughters to live and for them to visit.

Organization/Structure

The primary difference between living-learning units and cultural centers is the residential component. Many institutions with Native American living-learning units face a number of significant challenges, such as little institutional support and attracting or retaining Native students, faculty, and staff.

However, several institutions, such as Cornell University, Dartmouth College, the University of Arizona, and the University of Minnesota, have developed successful living units and cultural centers for Native American students. The creation of Native American residential units or LLPs on college campuses appears to have led to success in addressing the unique needs of Native American college students. Astin (1993) asserts that there is a need for cultural centers to promote a sense of belonging for minority students at NNCUs. To explore this further, Native American LLPs at two institutions, Cornell University and the State University of New York (SUNY) at Buffalo are presented as effective examples of such programs.

Native American Students at Cornell University

Cornell University, an Ivy League institution and New York's land-grant institution, located in Ithaca, New York, has a predominantly White student population of approximately 14,000. The Native American student population at the university is less than 200 and makes up approximately 1% of the total student population. Cornell is located on the ancestral homelands of the Cayuga Nation, a member of the Haudenosaunee, and is an hour from Onondaga. If one were to imagine a very large longhouse stretching across New York State from Albany to Buffalo, Onondaga—the political and spiritual seat—is at the center. Albany is traditionally Mohawk territory, between the Mohawk and Onondaga are the Oneida, then Cayuga, and Seneca territory near Buffalo. The Tuscarora joined the Haudenosaunee when they were driven from the Carolinas and are located near Niagara Falls.

American Indian Program

The American Indian Program (AIP) was formally established in 1983 as a result of the hard work of an ad hoc committee made up of Native American students, community members, faculty, and university administrators. In the early years, the AIP focused on recruiting Native students and providing student services. The AIP incorporates a full circle philosophy into its mission, which embodies three central components: (a) student services, (b) academics, and (c) outreach to Native American communities (AIP History, n.d.). The student services component includes recruitment and retention and the residential program house, Akwe:kon. It employs the "Three Rs: Recruitment, Retention, and Reintroduction into one's community" (AIP Full Circle Approach, 2010), as the AIP realizes that the success of the program is not in how many Native students the institution graduates, but how students are using their knowledge to give back to their community. The academic component provides an interdisciplinary Native American Studies minor. The outreach component focuses on outreach to Native American communities, often collaborating with Haudenosaunee communities on research projects with various communities throughout the state (AIP History, n.d.).

Akwe:kon

Owing to the perseverance of Ron LaFrance, director of the AIP from 1987 to 1994, Akwe:kon, the first university residence of its kind in the country, was opened on the Cornell campus in the fall of 1991. In the shape of an eagle, Akwe:kon was purposely built to celebrate Native American heritage and reflects thoughtful integration of Haudenosaunee symbols and traditions into the architecture and interior design. All exterior sides of the building are adorned with images of various Haudenosaunee wampum belts. Akwe:kon houses 35 students, half of whom are Native. The house has a great room for programming, a lounge furnished with a television and comfortable couches for residents, a fully functioning kitchen, a computer lab, administrative offices, and two guest rooms for visitors. The interior of Akwe:kon is adorned with various pieces of Native American art that have been donated to the house.

Located in the heart of North Campus, Akwe:kon serves as a student community center as well. Akwe:kon provides the building blocks for a close-knit community, and is much like an extended family for its residents, their families, and the larger Cornell and surrounding community. Since its inception in 1991, Akwe:kon has been the hub of Native American student life on campus. It regularly hosts many programs such as faculty fellow dinners to create sustained faculty interaction, field trips to neighboring Native communities and cultural centers, annual fry bread competitions, and student organizational meetings.

Although Akwe:kon primarily reflects Haudenosaunee culture, the architecture and philosophy of the house reflect communal values. Even the name of the house, Akwe:kon, meaning "all of us" in the Mohawk language, reflects inclusiveness with an emphasis on Native American culture. Over the past 20 years, Akwe:kon has become a touchstone for students on campus, serving as a home away from home, a safe haven, a place to reinforce Native values. It helps students foster a sense of belonging, which they do not necessarily feel in the larger campus community.

The University at Buffalo Jakonsase House

The University at Buffalo (UB) is a large Research I public university and one of the flagship institutions of SUNY. UB enrolls approximately 26,000 students, 16,000 of whom are undergraduates. At the time Jakonsase House was created, UB offered both graduate and undergraduate degrees in American studies with a minor in Native American Studies. Jakonsase is the name of the Seneca woman who first accepted the Peacemaker's message in Haudenosaunee tradition. A very prominent faculty included Haudenosaunee leaders and scholars such as John Mohawk, Barry White, Rick Hill, and Oren Lyons. Through the involvement of these faculty leaders, an undergraduate student association, the Native American People's Alliance (NAPA), was founded.

Geographically, UB also sits in Haudenosaunee territory. Nearby are the Seneca and Tuscarora reservations, and across the very close border of Canada is found the Six Nations Reserve. Given its location, within a relatively close distance are the Onondaga, Oneida, and Mohawk nations, and offerings, UB should be an institution Native Americans attend and where they succeed. Unfortunately, this was not the case in the early 1990s. During this time, college enrollments across the country were waning and fewer students were living in on-campus housing. The institution was challenged to create new housing options that would attract students who otherwise might not live on campus. Mike Gendrue, who is Native American and worked with the Native American students at the university, collaborated with the Residence Life Office to create a Native American living unit. He involved the president of NAPA, along with a graduate Native American student in the American studies program, Jason Harding. Together, they crafted a proposal to introduce a residential living unit to celebrate Native American culture.

The plan called for creating a living space on one floor to house approximately 20 students. The program would draw on the expertise of Akwe:kon at Cornell and other such programs. The first and most important challenge was to enlist the support of the students, all of whom lived off campus, in creating a space that would allow them to make a transition to living on campus. For these students, one of the most important obstacles was the cost of living on campus, which was substantially higher than living in an off-campus apartment or commuting from home. The advantages of living on campus for them would need to be significant and have benefits that could justify the additional cost. Also, to take full advantage of a space that was designed for single-gender occupancy, the program would need to house both men and women on the same floor. It was a traditional residence hall design with double rooms lining a hallway and a good-sized lounge space for students to gather. The plan called for a kitchen to be added to the lounge space so students could make their own food, traditional and other, and host programs that celebrated Native American culture on the floor, including dinners with the faculty and staff. Although the complexity and cost of these facility changes could be seen as a "nonstarter" for many housing programs, with the assistance of staff, faculty, and students, the director of residence life, Joe Krakowiak, became a supporter, and the necessary funding and design was achieved.

Working With University Administrators

One of the most difficult challenges and greatest opportunities is developing a compelling plan for creating a Native American residential living-learning program. To be successful, an understanding of the Native American student experience and the issues surrounding Native American higher education must be achieved. Many organizations are available to assist in educating campus administrators and others about the Native American student experience. The American Indian Graduate Center (AIGC), the National Institute for Native Leadership in Higher Education (NINLHE), the National Association for Student Personnel Administrators Indigenous Peoples Knowledge Communities (NASPA IPKC), and the American College Personnel Association Native American Network (ACPA NAN) are excellent resources for information on the Native American student experience. Too often, campus administrators dismiss the existence of Native American students because they represent a very small population at most NNCUs. For these campuses, it may be necessary to demonstrate the connection between establishing a Native American living community and recruiting Native American students to the campus. Many colleges and universities continue to be concerned with enrollments and are looking for creative ways to identify new avenues for recruitment. Developing a Native American recruitment plan that includes designated housing for Native American students and those students who are interested in Native American culture could produce untapped sources for student enrollment.

On campuses where cultural LLPs already exist, there may be an excellent opportunity to introduce a Native American residential program. Some campuses have not embraced the efficacy of LLPs. The challenges involved in establishing one may be rudimentary, but they may also present many exciting possibilities. Shapiro and Levine (1999) present a comprehensive guide for developing and implementing living-learning communities that may be particularly helpful in developing a plan or process to establish a Native American living-learning community.

Assessing the Campus Culture

It is necessary to understand the current level of awareness on campus with regard to Native American culture and the connected issues among faculty, staff, and administrators. Determining whether there is a Native American student organization or program that promotes Native American culture is a good first step. Also, looking for less obvious indications of the support for Native American culture, such as current and past relationships with local tribes, the history of land use by the college and the awareness of treaties governing local sovereignty issues, the overall campus commitment to the recruitment of Native American students in the college enrollment plan, and so on, will provide valuable insights into the process of establishing a Native American living-learning program.

Cultivating Partners

Identifying partners will be one of the most critical components in proposing the introduction of a Native American LLP. Stakeholders include the Native American students who currently attend the institution and those who are considering attending the institution, as well as their communities. Campus administrators who will be charged with implementing and running the program, such as the residence life staff, are also important stakeholders. Faculty who are Native American or who conduct research on Native American culture may also be interested in supporting the program. Finally, admissions officers are important as they can use the LLP as a recruitment tool.

Developing Curricula and Involving Faculty

On campuses where LLPs exist there may be a prescribed proposal process that includes a review by established committees at the institution. If this is not the case, it is important to consider whether the LLP will have a traditional curricular component. Involving supportive faculty in the proposal process is an important consideration. Many Native American residential programs have some curricular components, while others do not. Because of

Cornell's and UB's faculty, they were able to offer Haudenosaunee history and treaty classes.

Overcoming Logistical Challenges and Obstacles

There are many logistical considerations when establishing a Native American LLP. Is space available in the campus residence halls? Are there enough students to fill the residential space? Are there any existing policies that may be problematic? Are Native American students being recruited to the institution, and from what areas? Is there the opportunity to renovate the space to better accommodate Native American traditions and culture, and so on? Some of these issues may take several months or even years to address adequately, so it may be useful to keep this in mind when beginning the project and set expectations accordingly.

Developing Residential Programs

Introducing a Native American living unit on a campus that has existing LLPs is a great advantage, as the structure for program planning and funding often has already been developed. For campuses where the new Native American living unit is also introducing the living-learning concept, programming may add challenges that should be addressed as part of the overall program proposal. It is essential to have clear program expectations and probable funding sources included at the beginning of the process. Programming is also an important vehicle for supporting the participation of students and for raising awareness of Native American issues within the campus community.

In the living units developed, students may participate in programming requirements. For example, some living units are expected to provide two building-wide programs per semester. Examples of these programs have ranged from invited speakers such as the late Chief Wilma Mankiller of the Cherokee Nation to local tribal leaders who have spoken about current issues relating to federal law and treaties, as well as Native American scholars sharing their research. Programming has also included traditional socials and dinners to recognize student achievements. Socials are gatherings that feature Haudenosaunee social dancing and food. Programming such as this is an excellent opportunity to expand the unit's impact on the entire Native student community on campus.

Recommendations for Practitioners and Institutions

On the basis of our observations and experiences, we offer some recommendations to ensure the continued success of Native American LLPs and Native American students.

- Assessment of the experiences of students who have lived in Native American living units is needed and long overdue.
- Supportive programs that examine the development of living units for Native students should be developed by professional organizations such as the Association of College and University Housing Officials International (ACUHO-I), the American College Personnel Association (ACPA), and the National Association of Student Personnel Administrators (NASPA).
- It is important for any planned Native American living unit to be a part of a much larger and comprehensive plan for Native American student recruitment, support, retention, and ultimate success. However, the development of a living unit could serve as a catalyst for such a plan.
- Graduate preparation programs for future student affairs professionals must include curriculum and research to educate their students about Native American college student experiences and trends. Many of the students enrolled in these programs are currently serving in residence hall staff roles or are planning to serve in such roles.

Conclusion

Deloria and Wildcat (2001) asserted, "The thing that has always been missing in Indian education, and still is missing today, is Indians" (p. 152). For higher education in the United States, this continues to be a struggle with deep historical roots (Carney, 1999). The question, "Why don't more Native Americans attend college?" seems to be rooted in the old "chicken or egg" question: which comes first? How can colleges and universities expect to recruit and retain Native American students when they do not create environments that are culturally relevant for them, thus forcing these students to assimilate to be successful? As we can see from the following student quote, the creation of culturally relevant living spaces that promote a sense of belonging is crucial to student experiences:

The establishment of a Native American housing unit on campus brought together many students who were experiencing the same feelings I was. Although many of us grew up on reservations hundreds of miles apart, we bonded over having similar backgrounds and experiences. Many of us also expressed the same view: if it wasn't for the Native American Suite and each other for support, we would not have completed our degrees. We would have quit and gone back to our respective reservations and families, and ended up who-knows-where and doing who-knows-what. —Derwin (Mohawk)

Deloria and Wildcat (2001) provide a compelling plan to change higher education based on Indigenous models of education. But until this is accomplished, Native American students need colleges and universities to create a culturally relevant place for them, a place where they belong (Lowe, 2005). Native American residential living programs provide an excellent step in this direction and can be used to galvanize support for Native American students.

In this chapter, we have provided a foundation for creating residential living units for Native American students. Each campus is different and will have its own set of challenges and opportunities. Attempting to create these kinds of spaces on your campus will demonstrate your desire to "extend your rafters" and embrace these very important students.

References

AIP Full Circle Approach. (2010). Full circle approach. Retrieved December 1, 2011, from http://aip.cornell.edu/cals/aip/about/full-circle/index.cfm

AIP History. (n.d.). *American Indian program homepage.* Retrieved May 24, 2011, from http://aip.cornell.edu/cals/aip/about/history/index.cfm

Astin, A. W. (1993). Diversity and multiculturalism on campus: How are students affected? *Change, 25*(2), 44–49.

Barefoot, B. O. (2008). *The first year and beyond: Rethinking the challenge of collegiate transition.* San Francisco: Jossey-Bass.

Carney, C. M. (1999). *Native American higher education in the United States.* New Brunswick, NJ: Transaction.

Deloria, V., & Wildcat, D. R. (2001). *Power and place: Indian education in America.* Golden, CO: Fulcrum.

Ecklund, T. R. (2005). The relationship between psychosocial development and acculturation among American Indian college students. Ph.D. dissertation, State University of New York at Buffalo, New York. Retrieved January 5, 2009, from Dissertations & Theses: A&I database. (Publication No. AAT 3174142).

Garrod, A., & Larimore, C. (1997). *First person, first peoples: Native American college graduates tell their life stories.* Ithaca, NY: Cornell University Press.

HeavyRunner, I., & DeCelles, R. (2002). Family education model: Meeting the student retention challenge. *Journal of American Indian Education, 41*(2), 29–37.

Hurtado, S., Milem, J. F., Clayton-Pedersen, A., & Allen, W. R. (1996). Enhancing campus climates for racial/ethnic diversity: Educational policy and practice. In C. Turner, A. Lising Antonio, M. Garcia, B. Laden, A. Nora, & C. Presley (Eds.), *Racial and ethnic diversity in higher education* (pp. 671–684). Boston: Pearson Custom Publishing.

Inkelas, K., Soldner, M., & Szelényi, K. (2008). Living learning programs for first-year students. In W. Zeller (Ed.), *Residence life programs & the new student experience* (pp. 67–75). Columbia: University of South Carolina.

Inkelas, K., Szelényi, K., Soldner, M., & Brower, A. M. (2007). The national study of living-learning programs: 2007 report of findings. Retrieved December 1, 2011, from http://hdl.handle.net/1903/8392

Jackson, A. P., Smith, S. A., & Hill, C. L. (2003). Academic persistence among Native American college students. *Journal of College Student Development, 44*(4), 548–565.

Johnson, D. R., Soldner, M., Leonard, J. B., Alvarez, P., Inkelas, K. K., Rowan-Kenyon, H., & Longerbeam, S. (2007). Examining sense of belonging among first-year undergraduates from different racial/ethnic groups. *Journal of College Student Development, 48*(5), 525–542.

Lowe, S. C. (2005). This is who I am: Experiences of Native American students. In M. J. T. Fox, S. C. Lowe, & G. S. McClellan (Eds.), *New directions for student services: Serving Native American Students, 109*, 33–40. San Francisco: Jossey-Bass.

Min Lui, W., Cuyjet, M., & Lee, S. (2010). Asian American student involvement in Asian American cultural centers. In L. Patton (Ed.), *Cultural centers in higher education* (pp. 26–48). Sterling, VA: Stylus.

Patton, L. D. (2005). Power to the people!: A literature review of the impact of Black student protest on the emergence of Black cultural centers. In F. Hord (Ed.), *Black cultural centers and political identities* (pp. 151–163). Chicago: Third World.

Shapiro, N. S., & Levine, J. H. (1999). *Creating learning communities: A practical guide to winning support, organizing for change, and implementing programs.* San Francisco: Jossey-Bass.

Snyder, T. D., Tan, A. G., & Hoffman, C. M. (2006). *Digest of education statistics 2005* (NCES 2006-030). U.S. Department of Education, National Center for Education Statistics. Washington, DC: U.S. Government Printing Office.

Tierney, W. G. (1992). *Official encouragement, institutional discouragement: Minorities in academe—the Native American experience.* Norwood, NJ: Ablex.

Zeller, W. J. (2008). *Residence life programs and the new student experience.* Columbia, SC: National Resource Center for the First-Year Experience & Students in Transition.

4

THE HISTORICALLY NATIVE AMERICAN FRATERNITY AND SORORITY MOVEMENT

*Derek Oxendine (Lumbee), Symphony Oxendine (Cherokee/
Mississippi Choctaw), and Dr. Robin Minthorn (Kiowa/Apache/
Nez Perce/Assiniboine/Umatilla)*

H istorically Native American fraternities and sororities (HNAFS) were first established in the mid-1990s and have grown to seven organizations with representation on at least 25 campuses nationwide. Jahansouz and Oxendine (2008) first used the term *historically Native American fraternities and sororities* to refer to organizations that were founded on the principles of Native American cultural beliefs to serve Native American communities. The values of these organizations are to uphold tribal and Native American cultural beliefs as sacred. The creation of HNAFS stemmed from Native American students recognizing the importance of retention and support of Native students, a need for cultural awareness, and an opportunity to expand and promote the Native community on their respective campuses. In this chapter, we explore the foundation and growth of HNAFS and the emergence of these organizations within the context of the broader fraternity/sorority system. We also discuss the challenges these organizations face in their evolution, expansion, and relevance in both higher education and the Native American community. Last, we give recommendations for current and future professionals who work with HNAFS.

History

The origins of the American fraternity and sorority system can be traced directly, or indirectly, back to the late 1700s. Just as the broader fraternity and sorority system originated to fill the unmet needs of students, HNAFS also originated to fill a need. The first Native American Greek organization in the nation was Alpha Pi Omega Sorority, Inc., which was founded in 1994 at the University of North Carolina–Chapel Hill by four women known as the four winds. These women sought advice from elder women representing different Native tribes in North Carolina when exploring the idea of starting a sorority based on Native American traditions. The first American Indian fraternity, Phi Sigma Nu, was founded in 1996 at Pembroke State University (now the University of North Carolina–Pembroke) by eight young men to bring cohesion and self-reliance to Native men in college.

Since the founding of these two fraternal organizations, five others have emerged across the United States: Epsilon Chi Nu (East Carolina University, 1996); Sigma Omicron Epsilon (East Carolina University, 1997); Beta Sigma Epsilon (University of Arizona, 2001); Gamma Delta Pi (University of Oklahoma, 2001); and Omega Delta Psi (University of Northern Colorado, 2006). Each of these organizations has its own mission, purpose, traditions, and ceremonies that have been instilled to represent the founding members and the student population of their respective higher education institutions.

Modern fraternities and sororities can be traced to literary societies, also known as debating clubs, and are noted to have begun at Yale in 1753 (Rudolph, 1990). The evolution from literary societies to what we now know as fraternities and sororities was the direct result of the need to offer more support to and provide for broader socialization among students. With the rise of fraternities and sororities also came the formation of umbrella organizations, such as the National Panhellenic Conference (NPC) in 1902 for women's fraternities and sororities, and the North-American Interfraternity Conference (NIC) in 1909 for men's fraternities, to further the spirit of cooperation and shared standards (Anson & Marchesani, 1991).

In the beginning of the twentieth century, underrepresented students began to develop their own culturally based organizations. In 1906 Alpha Phi Alpha Fraternity, Inc., was founded at Cornell University, and the idea of Black fraternalism firmly took root. Since the formation of Alpha Phi Alpha, eight other fraternal organizations and an umbrella council, National Pan-Hellenic Council (NPHC), were founded for historically African American fraternities and sororities (Kimbrough, 2003). In 1904, at Louisiana State University, the Sociedad Hispano-Americana was established as a secret society for Spanish American students; in 1911 it became Sigma Iota Fraternity and later Phi Iota Alpha (Anson & Marchesani, 1991). The emergence of sustainable minority organizations such as Alpha Phi Alpha and Phi Iota Alpha, coupled with greater access to higher education, sparked an explosion of cultural and multicultural fraternities and sororities on campuses.

The majority of NIC and NPC groups have been established for well over a century, and most NPHC groups are fast approaching their centennial anniversaries. HNAFS are still in their infancy and have only begun to lay the foundation of what is to be their legacy. Unlike many of their first-year counterparts, Native American students do not arrive on college campuses with the notion of "going Greek." Generations of fraternity men or sorority women do not exist within Native families, unlike many of the non-Native students who actively seek out participation in Greek organizations on campus. In addition, there is a lack of knowledge of HNAFS within Indian Country, as they are not yet a firmly rooted tradition.

Foundations

The establishment of HNAFS grew out of the recognition of the unique needs of Native students on college campuses. Native American students recognized the importance of retention and support of Native students, a need for cultural awareness, and an opportunity to expand and promote the Native community on their respective campuses, and it was these major concepts that provided the foundation for HNAFS.

Retention

The founding members of HNAFS recognized the issues of attrition and retention of Native students that existed on their respective campuses, and all of the HNAFS founded at non-Native colleges and universities (NNCUs) have cited retention and attrition as the most significant reasons for their creation. At the time that the first HNAFS emerged, the trend in higher education for many institutions saw the implementation of blanket retention programs for students of color. However, these models marginalized Native American students by not recognizing, and failing to respond to, the significant diversity of students from separate and distinct tribal nations.

Despite administrators' efforts to develop these programs, there was a lack of knowledge regarding the needs of Native American students and the importance of kinship relationships among students. In response to this lack of administrative approaches, HNAFS were created as a student call to action to help combat the retention issues in culturally appropriate ways by including tribal traditions, values, and gender-specific roles that had been left out of retention models.

Support System

Owing to the small number of Native American faculty, staff, and students on many campuses, HNAFS were founded to provide representation and serve as a support system for Native students. The premise of providing a support network, or "family," within universities through the Greek system is not new or specific to HNAFS. For many students, the need for social support and connectivity is an important factor in a positive transition from home environments to the campus environment. Hurtado, Milem, Clayton-Pederson, and Allen (1999) found that minority students used a social support system to serve as a buffer and/or to solve academic difficulties, and that these social support networks increased minority students' satisfaction on their respective campuses.

Many Native students attending institutions of higher learning struggle with the transition from close-knit community home environments to the larger campus community at colleges and universities. Native American culture is deeply connected to relationships with others as well as a meaningful relationship to a place (Deloria &Wildcat, 2001). Therefore, it is imperative that Native students in higher education institutions are received into a positive, welcoming environment and allowed to incorporate their tribal and Native beliefs within the place of their higher education journey.

HNAFS help make the university community seem smaller by offering ways to engage with other Natives within the larger campus environment. The inclusion of elders in many of the organizations highlights the interrelatedness of Native American communities and the importance of maintaining ties while away from home. Inclusion of students' family, community, and culture is one of the strengths of HNAFS, in that it recognizes the whole student and positively influences his or her successful engagement on campus. It is vital to acknowledge and include families, communities, and the culture each student brings with him or her to ensure Native American student success and engagement on college campuses (Jackson & Smith, 2001; Jenkins, 1999; Tippeconnic Fox, Lowe, & McClellan, 2005).

Cultural Identity

While each institution may have a Native American student organization on campus, the HNAFS have provided a more intimate avenue to maintain and develop students' cultural beliefs. These organizations support the cultural identity development of members by bringing the elements of tribal culture and the importance of ceremony into the organizations. HNAFS were founded to serve a specific tribal affiliation, region of tribes, and/or local community. However, through growth and expansion, some have recognized the need to include an intertribal focus to accommodate the tribal diversity of their membership. Tierney (1999) notes that minority students whose ethnic identities are affirmed and honored on their campuses have a greater chance of completing their degrees. The uniqueness of HNAFS is that they reaffirm to students that they do not need to lose their cultural identity to be successful in college.

With respect to their Native American culture, Native American students enter college with varying degrees of identity development. By incorporating and practicing components of tribal culture, HNAFS can provide a cultural anchor to members who seek a greater knowledge of culture and tradition and continued ties to their home community and traditional ways of life to help establish and grow personal identity. For students who come from reservations or communities with strong connections to ceremonial and traditional ways of life, the HNAFS provide a sense of "home" by reaffirming and maintaining an identity they might not otherwise have on campus.

Each organization puts great emphasis on affirming and reinforcing cultural identity. For example, HNAFS use ceremonies, calls, strolls, dances, icons, colors, plants, jewels, and even hand signs based on certain tribal belief systems. While only organizational members know the significance and meaning of these symbols, their history and construction are highly influenced by generations of tribal practices. Among most of these organizations, elders and traditional people have been consulted during their founding and development to ensure that ceremonies and rituals are authentic and maintain traditional beliefs and practices.

Greek Model

Before creation of HNAFS, Native American students who wanted to be a part of the Greek experience had to choose to join organizations that were not culturally relevant, even though they may have been inclusive. Lack of inclusion of their Native American culture was the greatest reason many of the original founders of HNAFS chose not to join the organizations that existed at the time. The emerging HNAFS were founded with a basic understanding of how Greek organizations were structured and operated; however, this was done with minimal to no guidance. The founding members of HNAFS lacked knowledge of the larger interfraternal movement.

What the original founders used to begin successful implementation of HNAFS was their own resiliency and adaptability. These individuals represented tribal nations that have, since the time of first contact, met whatever challenges were before them and adapted the situation to meet their needs, thus finding ways to maintain their unique cultural identity. HNAFS used the positive aspects of Greek organizations and adapted them to meet their needs. However, by doing so, the founding members often faced opposition from their Native peers on campus and within their tribal communities, because Greek organizations in general were seen as foreign and as being "White" and not "Indian." Some even viewed a Native American Greek organization as yet another example of assimilation into mainstream culture.

The HNAFS founders saw things differently. They saw an opportunity to foster leadership development within their organizations. Most higher education institutions view the fraternity/sorority system as an experience that develops a student's leadership capacity. For founders of HNAFS, the potential for leadership development made the Greek organizational structure appealing. While there were other organizations in which Native American students could be involved on campus, they saw the Greek system as a way to highlight the fact that Native American students had the potential to be leaders within the larger campus community.

In spite of a lack of encouragement and assistance by student affairs administrators, and by adapting the Greek model but incorporating culture and traditional ceremony, the seeds for developing HNAFS were planted. The common perception of HNAFS by individuals, ranging from university administration to fraternity and sorority advising professionals, was that HNAFS are different and do not fit the mold of the larger fraternal community. Even though all HNAFS use Greek letters for naming the organization and have adopted some basic concepts of Greek organizations in terms of infrastructure (e.g., constitution, membership process, pledging, etc.), they still do not quite fit the fraternity/sorority mold because they incorporate Native American culture into how they operate and into their missions.

Valuing the culture, voice, and family of Native American students in higher education institutions supports the fundamental foundation of the seven HNAFS that currently exist in the United States. These tribal and cultural values represent the Native American student body at the respective higher education institution where each fraternity and sorority was founded. In addition to recognizing a need to create organizations to provide support and increase retention, the founding students wanted to create intimate and closer connections for students. These fraternities and sororities provide Native American college students with the opportunity to share with each other their tribal cultural values, learn from others, and create a stronger Native American community on campus.

Service

Another foundation of HNAFS is to provide service to the local communities and to those communities from which the students are drawn. HNAFS include and emphasize the importance of service in their organizations to maintain a connection with the local community and the university. Giving back is a strong value in many tribal cultures and serves as a source of motivation and persistence for many Native American college students (Guillory & Wolverton, 2008). Gamma Delta Pi, for example, honors the four stages of life—childhood, adolescence, adulthood, and old age—through community service that meets the needs of all four of these stages. It is also important for many HNAFS to be visible in giving back to their communities. By performing community service and addressing needs within tribal communities, these organizations have shown they are maintaining a relationship with Native culture and are gaining the respect of their tribal communities.

Evolution

HNAFS have experienced various stages of growth, and many have expanded to other campuses. Expansion of chapters of some HNAFS has occurred both at the state and national level. Through the growth in chapters nationwide and the expansion to regions where other tribal cultures are prominent, the evolution of fraternities/sororities has often incorporated the ceremonies and cultural values of the respective tribal cultures in that region. In turn, this integration and cultural representation by newly formed chapters has created a unique chapter culture within the sorority/fraternity while continuing to represent the founding organization in mission and purpose.

Additionally, as new chapters have formed and members have graduated, there has been a call to expand the HNAFS to include graduate and alumni/ae chapters within the organizations. This growth has allowed these chapters to contribute to the undergraduate chapters and to the organization as a whole in new and expanded ways. The establishment of scholarships, mentoring programs, and formal programs contributing to Native American issues locally and nationally has been a result of the postbaccalaureate portions of the HNAFS.

The growth of each organization is not necessarily measured in membership numbers. Rather, it is measured by a growing sisterhood or brotherhood that filters to chapters on other campuses. Evolution, growth, and expansion are also encompassed by new relationships and communities created in the growing bonds of sisterhood and brotherhood through ceremony and the sharing of tribal cultures and personal experiences.

Challenges

As with any emerging organization, obstacles can hinder growth and development, and HNAFS are no exception. There are currently several challenges that HNAFS must overcome, and these are critical to the future success of these organizations. In addition to these challenges, HNAFS have met with attitudes of disregard, lack of respect, and a sense of illegitimacy from the interfraternity movement.

Cultural Capital

Most HNAFS received little to no assistance from student organization and/ or fraternity and sorority advising professionals when establishing on college campuses. In general, there was an overall sense of discouragement in creating new organizations. Because many HNAFS lacked encouragement and guidance from key administrators during their founding, they were often created with only basic assumptions of how the Greek system worked. As interest and demand for new chapters increased, HNAFS quickly transformed from local to regional and/or national organizations. During this rapid expansion, many HNAFS realized they were deficient in their understanding of the fundamental practices and policies of the Greek system, particularly those requirements related to expanding their organizations to new campuses. As HNAFS continue to grow, they are faced with establishing governing alumni/national boards, creating organization-wide new member education and risk management policies, implementing membership standards, and purchasing national liability insurance. While several HNAFS have made progress in these areas, they remain a challenge for others.

Since the founding principles and values of HNAFS are built on traditions and cultures reflective of the tribal nations of Native students, they are held as sacred and spiritual and require respect and understanding. There is an educational and cultural awareness component that must be brought to Greek life departments, existing fraternities and sororities, and the greater campus community in institutions where HNAFS exist.

Social Capital

In 2007 HNAFS were first represented at the annual meeting of the Association of Fraternity/Sorority Advisors (AFA). At the 2008 AFA annual meeting, two HNAFS representatives were invited to take part in an interfraternal breakfast with the AFA Board of Directors and representatives from the six national umbrella organizations. This allowed HNAFS to emerge on the national scene of the fraternal movement.

For some campuses, current membership within a national umbrella organization is an institutional requirement for recognition on campus. However, membership in these national umbrella organizations is currently not an option for HNAFS as none of them meets the requirements for these groups in terms of membership numbers owing to their small size. As HNAFS continue to emerge on a local, regional, and national level, there is an increasing need to develop a network for communication, influence, and support. Such a collaborative network could provide a venue for development, mutual respect, and advocacy for HNAFS, in addition to promoting awareness of Native American culture and community. There have been informal discussions to establish a national Native American umbrella organization; however, HNAFS do not yet have the membership or financial resources to sustain both their individual organizations and a national umbrella organization.

Economic Capital and Sustainability

There are varying differences in the organizational development and evolution of HNAFS, with size playing a crucial role. For example, smaller organizations, such as Omega Delta Psi, Beta Sigma Epsilon, Sigma Omicron Epsilon, and Epsilon Chi Nu, focus the majority of their operations within their individual undergraduate chapters. In contrast, Gamma Delta Pi, Alpha Pi Omega, and Phi Sigma Nu, all of which have more members, have been able to implement governing alumni boards to oversee their undergraduate and graduate chapters, fiscal management, and expansion from a regional or a national perspective as an organization. However, owing to monetary constraints, these boards are all staffed by volunteers.

HNAFS range in size, with the smallest consisting of one chapter and the largest with 13 chapters; most chapters average six to eight members. When looking at the enrollment of Native American students in four-year institutions, and taking into account students who would be interested in joining an HNAFS organization, the numbers dwindle. The reality is these organizations will never boast hundreds of chapters or chapters consisting of 50+ members. However, for them to become more financially stable, they need to increase membership. In the interest of sustainability, HNAFS may have to find ways to increase membership without relying on undergraduate chapters. Several have implemented graduate chapters in the hopes of keeping alumni active and as a means to initiate interested professionals. Additional approaches to consider are developing a process for honorary membership and creating auxiliary groups. This could grow membership and increase representation and involvement in tribal communities to advance the ideals of HNAFS.

Economic capital and sustainability continue to be a challenge for HNAFS. Larger memberships would increase revenue to support chartering new chapters, provide opportunities for membership development, and purchase liability insurance. Most institutions require a liability insurance policy for Greek organizations to be recognized on campus. Thus far, obtaining insurance has not been an easy task for HNAFS. Three leading companies have monopolized the fraternal liability insurance market, and most HNAFS cannot afford coverage from these groups. Economic capitol and sustainability continue to be a challenge for HNAFS.

Recommendations for Practitioners and Institutions

As the evolution and growth of HNAFS continues, student affairs professionals and support staff need to be cognizant of and open to learning about these organizations. There can be hesitation in bringing HNAFS to campuses because student affairs professionals view them as a risk. It is important for these professionals to keep an open mind to the possibilities and strengths HNAFS can bring to the campus, Native American students, and the community.

One of the departments/offices HNAFS must work closely with is the Greek Affairs department, which serves the various sororities and fraternities on campus. It is important for Greek Affairs offices to be aware of current policies and practices and how they affect smaller organizations, especially culturally based organizations. Key policies governing the recognition process, such as requirements for membership size, academics, and level of participation, have affected HNAFS. The founding purpose and size of HNAFS organizations have an impact on their ability to comply with such policies. Therefore, supporting and promoting HNAFS on university and college campuses and affording them equal opportunity to highlight the organization is essential.

It is imperative that Native American higher education professionals understand their role in advocating for the HNAFS on campus, to help foster relationships with Greek Affairs departments, and to provide a voice for the Native American culture and community on campus. In our experience, cultural revitalization and growth is often seen in Native American students who choose to participate in HNAFS. Therefore, it is important for non-Native professionals to gain the support of the Native American higher education professionals on campus, if there are any, to help identify ways in which these organizations can flourish and grow.

As HNAFS appear on university and college campuses, Greek Affairs professionals should be aware of biased and culturally inappropriate terminology that can be offensive to HNAFS and other culturally based organizations on campus. Building bridges between various councils and Greek organizations is important and imperative to the success of HNAFS, as is building relationships and cultural awareness within the Greek and campus community.

Institutional support has played an important role in the founding of HNAFS. Some chapters were founded in spite of a lack of encouragement by institutions and administrators, and some have flourished because of institutional advocacy. Backing by the university president and other administrators should play a role in promoting the importance of culturally based organizations such as HNAFS. Institutional policies and practices should be explored and modified to be inclusive and respectful of HNAFS ceremonies and rituals as they emerge on university and college campuses. Institutional requirements for recognition as a Greek organization often create an undue burden for HNAFS and should be evaluated. Moreover, the need for cultural awareness, education, and competency should be incorporated by the university administration and Greek Affairs departments to foster a better understanding of the strengths HNAFS and other culturally based organizations bring to the entire campus community.

Conclusion/Future Outlook for Historically Native American Fraternities and Sororities

As the number of Native American students in higher education continues to grow, the demand for HNAFS on campuses is likely to increase. In addition, the diversity of Native America presents a great opportunity for students to have cross-cultural interactions and to share their culture in progressive and intimate ways with fellow organization members and the greater community. However, to sustain growth, HNAFS must maintain a relationship with the broader fraternal community. By tapping into the trends and issues affecting the larger fraternal community, they can meet and address these within their own organizations and stay current with developments within the larger Greek community. While HNAFS should be aware of the broader issues affecting the fraternity and sorority community, there should be some consideration about whether the fraternal movement is actually relevant to HNAFS, because to take a seat at the fraternal community table, HNAFS must make themselves known and visible in a way that is respectful of Native cultural values.

HNAFS serve a very important purpose for their members. They have an impact on the campuses and in the communities where they are located. It is important to understand that these organizations were founded to fill a gap within the Native American student community on college campuses. HNAFS organizations are unique in many ways and this uniqueness should not be confused with legitimacy or the impact these organizations can have within both the Greek system and the broader Native American community.

Note: The authors have been a part of the Native American fraternal values movement as members, advisors, and advocates and have provided their experiences and insight and those shared by their fellow HNAFS members.

References

Anson, J. L., & Marchesani, R. F., Jr. (Eds.). (1991). *Baird's manual of American college fraternities* (20th ed.). Indianapolis, IN: Bairds Manuel Foundation, Inc.

Deloria, V., & Wildcat, D. (2001). *Power and place: Indian education in America.* Golden, CO: Fulcrum Resources.

Guillory, R., & Wolverton, M. (2008). It's about family: Native American student persistence in higher education. *Journal of Higher Education, 79*(1), 58–87.

Hurtado, S., Milem, J., Clayton-Pederson, A., & Allen, W. (1999). *Enacting diverse learning environments: Improving the climate for racial/ethnic diversity in higher education*. ASHE-ERIC Higher Education Report, *26*(8). Washington, DC: George Washington University, Graduate School of Education and Human Development.

Jackson, A. P., & Smith, S. A. (2001). Postsecondary transitions among Navajo students. *Journal of American Indian Education, 40*(2), 28–47.

Jahansouz, S., & Oxendine, S. (2008, Spring). The Native American fraternal values movement: Past, present, & future. *Perspectives*, 14.

Jenkins, M. (1999). Factors which influence the success or failure of American Indian/Native American college students. *Research and Teaching in Developmental Education, 15*(20), 49–52.

Kimbrough, W. M. (2003). Black Greek 101: The culture, customs, and challenges of Black fraternities and sororities. Madison, NJ: Fairleigh Dickinson University Press.

Rudolph, F. (1990). *The American college and university: A history*. Athens: University of Georgia Press.

Tierney, W. G. (1999). Models of minority college-going and retention: Cultural integrity versus cultural suicide. *The Journal of Negro Education, 68*, 80–91.

Tippeconnic Fox, M. J., Lowe, S. C., & McClellan, G. S. (2005). From discussion to action. In M. Fox, S. Lowe, & G. McClellan (Eds.), *Serving Native American students* (pp. 95–98). San Francisco: Jossey-Bass.

5

THE ROLE OF THE SPECIAL ADVISOR TO THE PRESIDENT ON NATIVE AMERICAN AFFAIRS

Karen Francis-Begay (Diné)

Arizona sits in the heartland of the southwest and is home to 22 federally recognized tribes, which make up 4% of the state's population and control approximately 32% or 38,677 square miles of the state's land base. The University of Arizona (UA) is a land-grant, public, Research I university with 38,767 students (UA Office of Institutional Research & Planning Support, 2010b). It was founded in 1885 on what is the historical homeland of the O'odham people (previously called Papago, descendants of the ancient Hohokam). The campus now covers 387 acres in central Tucson and brings in $530 million in research funding. The UA is ranked second highest in the nation for producing the most graduate degrees for Native Americans in engineering and ethnic, cultural, and gender studies (UA Office of Communications, 2010).

The Native American student presence at the UA is significant when compared to that at other public, research universities. When self-identifying as Native American, students do not have to verify tribal authenticity and/ or enrollment unless scholarships require verification. The first-to-second-year persistence rates for first-time, full-time freshmen has averaged 63.8% over a 10-year period from 1990 to 2008 (UA Office of Institutional Research & Planning Support, 2010b). In 2008 the proportion of administrators and faculty who identified as American Indian or Alaska Native was 0.2%, while 0.7% of classified staff identified as American Indian or Alaska Native (UA Office of Institutional Research & Planning Support, 2010b).

In 1999 the University of Arizona created a position to advise the university president on issues relevant to Native American communities and to serve as an advocate for students. The UA was not the first to take this important step; several other public state universities have also created a tribal liaison position. The Montana State University, University of Idaho, University of New Mexico, Washington State University, University of Oregon, Northern Arizona University, and Arizona State University also have tribal liaisons or special advisors who have been appointed within the last 10 years. This chapter begins by highlighting a few of the many Native American programs and services at the UA. A discussion follows on the development of the special advisor position and its role on campus and the opportunities and challenges of the position. The chapter concludes with recommendations for university administrators to consider when creating a tribal liaison position at their institution.

The University of Arizona's History of Native American Support

The UA has several outstanding student and academic programs geared toward access for and success of Native American students. The Native American student affairs (NASA) office, currently housed in the Dean of Students Office, serves as the primary support program for Native American students. NASA works with several offices to provide support for Native students and is home of the Wassaja Student Center and the First-Year Scholars Program (discussed in chapter 1).

In 1982 the Office of Student Financial Aid (OSFA) designated one of its counselors to work with Native American students to ensure a level of consistency and efficiency of services. Working with tribally based funding sources can create many challenges for students because tribes operate on a different fiscal year from the UA. For example, scholarship distributions often arrive mid-semester after student tuition and residential fees are due, creating increased financial obstacles for students. The OSFA addresses this by providing a counselor to work with Native American students and families and with the NASA office to offer additional funding resources for students such as short-term loans or emergency grants.

The Office of Admissions' efforts to recruit Native American students have historically been positive and have resulted in a steady increase of enrollment over the last 20 years. Competitive admission criteria and increasing tuition have not deterred Native American students from applying to the university in large numbers. The 2010 fall term had more than 200 freshmen enrolled, the largest class ever (UA Office of Institutional Research & Planning Support, 2010b). The more recent enrollment increases may be attributed to having a full-time, Native American admissions counselor based in northern Arizona to provide students, families, high school counselors, and teachers with application information and other resources. Recruitment scholarships, both merit- and need-based, may also contribute to increasing enrollment.

Academically, the university has national and international recognition for its programs in American Indian studies (AIS), law, and education. These programs have helped boost graduate student enrollment numbers primarily owing to the distinction and prestige of its Native American faculty. Established in 1982, the AIS program has three areas of concentration: Native American literature, law and policy, and education. The program also offers a joint MA/JD degree. The College of Law has a strong Indigenous Peoples Law and Policy (IPLP) Program for students who want to gain an in-depth understanding of global issues affecting Indigenous Peoples and communities. Another program of international focus is the American Indian Language Development Institute (AILDI), affiliated with both the College of Education and AIS. AILDI is a four-week, intensive summer program for educators, scholars, and students who have an interest in language preservation and curriculum development. The program has made a valuable contribution to protecting and preserving tribal/Indigenous languages.

The UA prides itself on its outreach to tribal communities. Several departments have years of experience in the field working and consulting with tribes on a variety of projects. The Arizona State Museum, for example, has a number of educational programs to promote tribal heritage and history. A popular event sponsored annually by the museum is the Southwest Indian Art Fair (SWIAF), for which over 100 Native American artisans are invited to showcase and sell their artwork. The museum also has a team of archeologists who conduct fieldwork in consultation with tribal communities and enforce federal policies such as the Native American Graves Protection and Repatriation Act (NAGPRA).

Well known for their expertise in medicine, the UA health sciences have a strong outreach component to serve tribal nations. The Native American Research and Training Center (NARTC) in the Department of Family and Community Medicine contributes extensively to increasing awareness and research on diabetes and has developed resource material for tribes and health organizations on diabetes prevention. The College of Medicine prides itself on its telemedicine program, which provides services to reservation communities and rural health centers. The Arizona Cancer Center recently renewed a grant from the National Cancer Institute (NCI) for the Native American Cancer Partnership Program to increase research and education about cancer for Arizona's tribal communities.

Other notable outreach projects extend beyond the region and state. The Native Nations Institute (NNI) for leadership, management, and policy provides tribal communities with leadership training and resource material on Native nation building. The American Indian Alumni (AIA) organization, also active in student recruitment, seeks to enhance its network capacity, raise funds for student scholarships, and provide a mentoring network to current students.

History of the Special Advisor

Before 2006 the special advisor position was an affiliate position referred to as the associate to the president for American Indian affairs and ambassador to American Indian nations. Dr. Mary Jo Tippeconnic Fox (Comanche) assumed the position, which reported directly to then-president Dr. Peter Likins, while also serving as department head of American Indian Studies. The scope of the position was outlined in a July 1999 letter (to the UA campus community) from President Likins:

> [T]here are more than twenty separate programs or organizations at the UA for Native Americans or American Indians, many of them functioning very effectively in some sector of the university, and these will continue their separate operations. Several of these programs are quite active in the tribal communities, playing important roles in such fields as health care and agriculture.
>
> Dr. Fox will play a new role in connecting each of these programs with the office of the university president and thereby strengthening their interconnections. She will serve as a single point of contact for American Indians on campus or in the tribal communities who need help in accessing available university programs and other resources. (UA College of Agriculture, 1999)

President Likins, who foresaw the benefits of having an ambassador to tribal nations at a public, land-grant university situated in a state with 21 federally recognized tribes, explored having a tribal liaison for the university. When President Likins resigned his term as president of the UA, Dr. Fox stepped down from her role as ambassador. Because I had been mentored by Dr. Fox throughout my directorship of the NASA office, she put forward my name for consideration to be the new tribal liaison for the incoming president, Dr. Robert Shelton. On July 1, 2005, I was appointed special advisor to the president on American Indian affairs ("American Indian" later changed to "Native American" after tribal leaders opposed use of the term *Indian*) while also serving as the full-time NASA director.

The UA president's American Indian Advisory Council (AIAC) (again "American Indian" would be replaced with "Native American"), established in 2005 by President Shelton, is made up of the highest elected leaders from six tribes in Arizona, Arizona's two tribal college presidents, several community leaders, and two student representatives. The council's charge is to provide advisement to the president on workforce development, student recruitment and retention, and research. On September 21, 2006, the AIAC presented President Shelton with a report, *Recommendations to the President in Support of American Indian Student Communities*, outlining key priorities, recommendations, and strategies to advance mutually beneficial initiatives between tribes and the university. Using supporting data and documentation from the university and outside sources, the AIAC identified four priority areas and recommendations outlined in Table 5-1.

TABLE 5-1
Recommendations to the President in Support
of Native American Student Communities

Priority	Recommendation
Tribal partnerships	Appoint a full-time tribal ambassador to strengthen partnerships with tribes to achieve mutual goals.
Student recruitment	Increase recruitment of Native American students to represent the diversity of the state of Arizona.
Student retention	Establish a formal commitment of university departments and programs to improve retention and graduation rates of Native American students.
Research in Native American communities	Increase opportunities for faculty and students to learn about research in tribal communities.

On August 24, 2007, President Shelton appointed me as the full-time special advisor to the president for American Indian affairs, a move that was monumental for the UA. As I settled into my new position, the assistant director for NASA was appointed interim director, and I moved into an office in the administration building (often referred to as the institution's "Ivory Tower"), which placed me in closer proximity to the president's office. Anticipating that I would have to deal with many campus and community requests, I hired a consultant to help me develop a strategic plan. This task was important as it enabled me to identify and prioritize needs and come up with a plan outlining measurable goals and objectives.

Appointing a full-time special advisor demonstrated the UA's commitment to understanding and valuing tribal sovereignty. The institution has enhanced many of its programs and services targeting Native Americans with the understanding that these programs benefited not a "minority" group or "race," but a multitude of individual and uniquely sovereign tribal nations. Native Americans who are members of federally recognized tribes hold separate and unique political and legal classifications. Many of our Native American students come from tribal communities that have their own form of government, language, cultural customs, and values. The leaders of these tribal nations embody power and authority similar to leaders from other countries. The UA acknowledges the uniqueness of tribal nations and honors government-to-government negotiations and agreements. The special advisor to the president on American Indian affairs is needed not only to serve as a liaison with the tribes in the state of Arizona, but also to work with out-of-state tribes and organizations that have a vested interest in the university.

Two years after my appointment, President Shelton made another important appointment in the area of diversity. He appointed the director of the Diversity Resource Office (DRO) to be a special advisor to the president on diversity and inclusion. Before the appointment, the director of DRO reported to the vice president for academic affairs. The UA was moving forward on many of its diversity initiatives, particularly with a focus on hiring and retaining faculty of color. The DRO was renamed the Office of the Special Advisor on Diversity and Inclusion and was relocated from a dilapidated building to the administration building. The main focus of the office is to promote diversity initiatives on campus and to serve as a liaison to the different diversity groups both on and off campus.

The Office of the Special Advisor on Diversity and Inclusion also supports the president's six different community advisory boards, which focus on issues affecting the African American, Native American, Hispanic, Asian/

Pacific American, disability, and lesbian/gay/bisexual/transgendered/queer (LGBTQ) communities. I assist the special advisor on diversity and inclusion with the Native American Advisory Council by communicating with the council membership, setting meetings and agendas, and preparing reports. Overall, our partnership promotes the university's diversity agenda.

In fulfilling the UA's role as a land-grant institution, President Shelton understood that the university must demonstrate its inclusivity of tribal nations in the state of Arizona. Arizona has the third-largest American Indian population in the United States (U.S. Census Bureau, 2002). In addition, Arizona tribes play a significant role in the state's economy with diverse economic enterprises, including but not limited to gaming, natural resource management, tourism, retail, and cultural art. There are also two tribal colleges, Diné College and Tohono O'odham Community College, that educate and provide a skilled workforce and prepare students for transfer to a university.

Role of the Special Advisor

In my role as special advisor to the president on Native American affairs, I serve as a critical liaison between the UA and tribes to strengthen partnerships and advance mutual goals. As the primary contact and resource on Native American affairs for the president and cabinet, I provide leadership in the enhancement of public relations work with national, state, and tribal entities. The position is vital to strengthening the visibility and presence of the UA among tribal nations and for collaborating with university officials, academic colleges, and departments on new initiatives related to outreach, partnership, development, policy, and research.

In the development of the strategic plan, several priorities were outlined to guide my role in this position. The UA Five-Year Strategic Plan for 2008–2011 was a key consideration in the development of my plan, as were the recommendations put forth by the UA president's Native American Advisory Council. After consultation with President Shelton on the plan, the following guiding principles were finalized: (a) strengthen the visibility and presence of the UA among tribal nations through outreach and collaboration; (b) raise awareness and develop understanding of tribal governance, enterprises, culture, and customs among university administrators, faculty and staff; and (c) develop opportunities in support of American Indian student recruitment, retention, and graduation. Following are examples and an explanation of each goal.

- **Strengthen the visibility and presence of the UA among tribal nations through outreach and collaboration:** The UA recognizes and supports the sovereign status of tribes and their government-to-government relationship with the United States. Tribal consultation and collaboration in key areas, such as tribal/university relations, economic development, academics, student recruitment and retention, cultural protection and preservation efforts, and research, are critical to fostering positive relations and achieving shared goals.

One strategy to strengthen the visibility and presence of the UA among tribal nations is to arrange visits for the president with tribal leaders in their respective tribal communities. President Shelton visited at least four different tribal communities in two years, some for a second or third time. The benefits of these visits are multifaceted. The president and members of his cabinet gain anawareness of the tribal community's challenges while appreciating the community's pride in and emphasis on retaining language and culture.

In all cases, there is important dialogue, not only among the leadership, but also with the governing tribal council. These visits and meetings provide a forum to exchange information on how partnerships can be formed to support the tribe's progress toward economic self-sufficiency and degree attainment. In addition to official business, the university visitors are usually welcomed and greeted by tribal elders and spiritual leaders before enjoying a cultural presentation and meal.

- **Raise awareness and develop understanding of tribal governance, enterprises, culture, and customs among university administrators, faculty, and staff.** The UA engages in a multitude of activities that directly and tangentially affect tribal nations and communities. Partnerships, community relations, and communication can be strengthened when respect, knowledge, and sensitivity are present within the university campus community.

To accomplish this strategy, the UA hosted a regional summit that brought together tribal leaders and university administrators to engage in dialogue about creating partnerships to promote Native American student success. Hosted at the UA campus in partnership with the President's Office of the UA, Chancellor's Office of Pima Community College, President's Office of Tohono O'odham Community College, and the Inter Tribal

Council of Arizona, Inc., "Partnering to Assist Native American Students to Access, Persist, and Succeed in Higher Education" took place on October 19, 2009. With nearly 250 participants representing tribal education departments in Arizona and New Mexico, Native American student organizations, K–12 school districts, tribal colleges, community colleges, and state university personnel, the summit's overall goal was to address the importance of partnerships and collaborations between tribes and higher learning institutions in support of Native American students. The summit recommendations continue to guide our efforts to improve Native American student access and success in postsecondary education.

• **Develop opportunities in support of Native American student recruitment, retention, and graduation.** Through coordinated partnerships with university administrators and programs, and tribal leaders and education departments, targeted efforts will be made to support Native American students through fund-raising, tribal outreach, and advocacy.

The UA implemented this strategy by becoming a key partner in and leader of the Arizona Tri-Universities for Indian Education (ATUIE) organization. With encouragement by the Fort McDowell Yavapai Nation, the ATUIE was officially formed on November 17, 2000, and soon after the state's two tribal colleges joined the organization. The mission of ATUIE is to lead the nation in Native American student recruitment, retention, and graduation; advocate and support Native American leadership at the highest levels within the state universities, colleges, and tribal governments; and support integration of both academics and culture for the total well-being of its students. Its goals fall into three areas: student services, self-sufficiency, and policy development and advocacy. The organization serves as a model for statewide coalition building for Native American higher education.

Opportunities and Challenges

There are many opportunities and challenges in my role as the special advisor to the president on Native American affairs. I have met with several of my counterparts on occasion and have learned that we all have similar challenges in the work we do. One challenge is the need to continually educate the campus community about Native Americans and to serve as the spokesperson for *all* tribes. A second challenge is to find a balance in how you deal with the many issues that come to your attention because of your close association with the president. Another challenge is dealing with the political dynamics of our work. We frequently engage with many tribal, state, federal, and nonprofit entities, as well as with our own internal constituents (faculty, administrators, staff, and students). Regardless of the challenges we face, it is important to have a strategy and a plan that outline your specific goals and objectives.

I've never been comfortable with politics, but it is an essential part of my work. I have practiced a great deal of diplomacy and patience in my work with tribal leaders and tribal organizations, no matter what issue we are addressing. I think being Native American is a benefit in my role as it gives me the background and understanding needed to address some of the complexities that exist in building and maintaining trust and relationships with tribal nations. It can be challenging at times to represent a state university system because tribes are cautious and have not always been trusting of government agencies, such as state universities. The heart of this work lies in having Native American students' best interests at heart when working with the tribal communities, parents, students, tribal education departments, teachers, principals, tribal councils, or leaders of tribal nations.

Another opportunity and challenge is in policy development and implementation. The tri-university system is engaged in developing a tribal consultation policy that will support and strengthen the new and long-standing practices of many of the UA programs that work with tribal nations. This policy will incorporate significant components, such as guiding principles, research, education and training, and enforcement. All three universities will work in partnership with the leadership of Arizona's tribal nations to develop the policy. There are, however, significant challenges to engaging all 22 tribes of Arizona in this important policy development endeavor. For example, some tribes have developed their own research policies and others have not, and yet research is a significant component of the tribal consultation policy. It will take some time before we have a consensus on this policy given the wide variation of interests and recommendations (by the universities and tribes) that need to be taken into account as the policy is created.

A final opportunity and challenge is continuing to enhance the value and significance of the special advisor role on campus. There should be opportunities for the special advisor to become part of broader governance committees and councils that have decision- and policy-making power. The three-year strategic plan aligns the special advisor's roles and responsibilities with the broader strategic plan of the institution. However, there will continue to be questions about the role of the position because it is unique and it encompasses a wide range of responsibilities. Its significance and success must coincide with the president's commitment to serving the needs of tribal nations.

Recommendations

Based on my own experiences, I've come up with a few recommendations that advance the visibility and importance of the special advisor role. First, relationship building is a key skill for the special advisor. I value and respect the fact that tribal leaders deal with many complicated issues daily, and everyone's time is valuable. It takes considerable patience and consistent outreach to create successful partnerships between the university and tribes, and follow-up is critical. Nobody wants short-lived or unfulfilled commitments. Long-term relationships are valued as is the ability to provide sustainable services and programs. The special advisor plays a key role in maintaining successful relationships with tribes while being an ambassador for the university.

There is a tremendous need for more high-level Native American administrators and faculty at colleges and universities across the country. It is important that university presidents are committed to increasing the representation of administrators and faculty of color. Resources need to be allocated to enhance recruitment efforts for top-level positions and to recruit outstanding faculty. There is also a need to increase the talent pool and support students of color aspiring to complete doctoral degrees and compete for tenure-track faculty or top-level administrative positions. The special advisor has the ability to identify a strong talent pool and make Native American faculty and administrator recruitment and retention a top priority for the university.

Finally, tribes are hesitant to engage with research institutions if trust has been breached. Tribal nations value respectful and meaningful consultation and request that this take place prior to formal agreements between the university and tribes. Recent distrust of university research has occurred because university researchers have violated tribal and institutional research protocol, which has resulted in minimal, if any, sanctions imposed on the researcher. Many funding agencies support research in tribal communities, yet the tribes often are not consulted before a researcher submits a research grant that involves them. Tribes want to be a partner when research projects involve their members or communities as they are the bearers of knowledge about the community and ultimately know what is in the best interest of the tribe. All postsecondary institutions should consider developing some type of tribal consultation policy to guide universities in working with tribes, bearing in mind that the most important element of policy development pertaining to tribes is developing the policy *with* the tribes, not *for* the tribes. The special advisor plays a vital role in arranging tribal consultation meetings that allow all stakeholders to share their concerns and come to a consensus before any further action is taken. Such consultation benefits everyone while also promoting and protecting important relationships.

Conclusion

The special advisor to the president on Native American affairs is an important position for any mainstream university that aspires to increase Native American student enrollment and graduation rates. The position plays a significant part in developing and enhancing relationships between the institution and tribal communities. We need more Native American professionals in higher education who can advocate for and lead their communities. In addition, it is evident that we need more research by Native Americans that portrays their personal stories and experiences in higher education. We need to continue to find ways to improve educational opportunities for Native students so they can be the leaders of tomorrow. Tribal nations cannot operate in isolation; partnerships are key to their future and success. The highest levels of university leadership must demonstrate a commitment to improving access and success for Native students. Without this commitment, we go nowhere. As a Navajo saying goes, "*T'áá shí 'ánísht'eego t'éiyá 'ádoolnííl*" (If it has to be, it is up to me). I live by this saying and will continue to dedicate my lifetime to Native American education. I hope others will be inspired by the path I have followed in my own journey, and can learn and benefit from my professional and personal experiences in higher education.

References

The University of Arizona (UA), College of Agriculture. (1999). Other resources for Indian students at the University of Arizona. *Arizona Land and People*, *47*(2). Retrieved from http://ag.arizona.edu/pubs/general/azlp47-2/other_resources.html

The University of Arizona (UA) Office of Communications. (2010). UA ranks nationally in graduating diverse students. Retrieved July 23, 2010, from http://uanews.org/node/32949

The University of Arizona (UA) Office of Institutional Research & Planning Support. (2009). *The University of Arizona fact book 2008–09*. Tucson, AZ: Author.

The University of Arizona (UA) Office of Institutional Research & Planning Support. (2010a). *First-time, full-time freshmen persistence and graduation rates [Data file]*. Retrieved from http://oirps.arizona.edu/files/Student_Demo/Compendium/FR_FTFT_NA_Table.pdf

The University of Arizona (UA) Office of Institutional Research & Planning Support. (2010b). *UA minority student enrollment trends, fall 1983 to fall 2009 [Data file]*. Retrieved from http://oirps.arizona.edu/files/Student_Demo/Enrollment_trends_for_minority_students_1983_2009.pdf

U.S. Census Bureau. (2002). The American Indian and Alaska Native population: 2000. Washington, DC: Author.

6

TRIBAL COLLEGE
COLLABORATIONS

Dr. Justin Guillory (Nez Perce Descendant)

A s a higher education professional, how many times have you heard the following comments?

- "We would like to partner with you."
- "Our president said we need to collaborate with you more."
- "I heard about your program and I think we would make a good partner."
- "We are submitting a grant proposal and wanted to know if you would be willing to partner with us."

Perhaps you are in a position where you receive these types of questions or solicitations regularly. Have you ever wondered why some partnerships work and others do not? What is the difference? What makes some collaborations successful and others miss the mark?

Now, imagine if you were entrusted with the task of collaborating with a tribal college. Where would you begin? What approach or strategy would you use? What are the benefits of collaborating with a tribal college? Developing a strong, collaborative partnership with any college or university can be complex, and tribal college collaborations are no different. In the fast-paced world of higher education with limited resources, heavy workloads, and shifting interests, the notion of a strong, mutually beneficial partnership between and among colleges and universities is becoming more and more challenging. Despite this challenging climate, establishing partnerships is becoming a necessity in light of today's economy. Make no mistake: the economy affects everyone and virtually every institution. This trend will ultimately result in greater interest in and need for collaborations across the higher education spectrum, including between tribal colleges and universities (TCUs) and mainstream institutions.

As colleges and universities are being asked to do more with less, by engaging in the arduous task of reprioritizing and realigning themselves while staying true to their respective missions, current approaches to collaborations, partnerships, and relationship building can no longer be business as usual. Partnerships, if they are to achieve their full potential, cannot afford to be superficial or based on convenience, and they certainly cannot be motivated by self-interest. Collaborations today must make the needs and interests of both parties the highest priority in order to optimize the worth and benefits such collaborations promise.

The purpose of this chapter is to provide mainstream student affairs professionals with practical strategies and approaches on how to collaborate and partner with TCUs. It explores and provides insights into questions such as: What are the benefits of collaborations? What lessons can be learned from previous collaborations between tribal and mainstream institutions? What are the barriers to collaborations? Finally, this chapter includes practical recommendations on how TCUs and nontribal institutions can build collaborative partnerships.

History of Tribal College Collaborations

Since the first TCUs emerged in the late 1960s, they have been engaged in collaborations with mainstream institutions. In their early years, tribal college collaborations were motivated by the desire of TCU leaders and elders to become accredited institutions of higher education (Nichols & Monette, 2003). To accomplish this, they forged partnerships with two- and four-year degree institutions to offer courses leading to an accredited degree. TCUs needed non-Indian colleges and universities to sponsor their institutions and accept their students' credits (Boyer, 1995). For TCUs, the primary motivation for entering into partnerships with mainstream institutions was eventually to become accredited institutions of their own. However, while TCU leaders actively sought partnerships with their mainstream counterparts, they also had no desire to remain dependent on these mainstream institutions.

Today, the majority of TCUs offer two-year degrees and an increasing number now offer baccalaureate and master's degrees (Stein, 2009). Achieving land-grant status in 1994, TCUs have become leaders in areas such as culturally relevant teaching and learning practices, place-based education, and research using methodologies and practices that directly benefit tribal communities. As a result, TCUs have been attractive to mainstream institutions and those that seek the value-added element TCUs can provide as potential partners with similar interests.

What Is Unique About a Tribal College?

Although TCUs vary considerably, they share some general characteristics that distinguish them from nontribal institutions. The core mission and identity of TCUs can be described as *nation building*, the rebuilding of Indigenous nations through the teaching of tribal histories, languages, and cultures (Crazy Bull, 2009). TCUs have a dual mission: cultural preservation and revitalization and a focus on Western models of learning that provide mainstream disciplinary courses and degrees that can be transferred to mainstream four-year or graduate institutions (American Indian Higher Education Consortium [AIHEC] & Institute for Higher Education Policy [IHEP], 1999; Stein, 2009). TCUs also focus on bridging historical and contemporary knowledge in a cultural context. Most TCUs are located on rural Indian reservations, began as two-year institutions, are less than 40 years old, have relatively small student bodies (often fewer than 500 students) that are predominantly American Indian, are chartered by one or more tribes, and have open admissions policies (Boyer, 1997; AIHEC & IHEP, 1999).

Other distinguishing characteristics of TCUs are their history and origin. They were founded by Indian people for Indian people on the basis of tribal sovereignty and treaty rights. Tribal sovereignty refers to the inherent sovereignty of tribal nations and their right to self-governance, self-determination, and self-education (Lomawaima, 1999; Lomawaima & McCarty, 2002). The U.S. government signed legal and binding treaties with American Indian tribes (Horse, 2005) confirming their legal and political status. TCUs, which are chartered by tribal governments just as mainstream public higher education institutions are chartered by state governments, are an example of tribal sovereignty. As another example of tribal sovereignty, each college embodies and promotes the unique culture of the tribe it serves.

Though initially modeled after and similar to mainstream community colleges, TCUs are fundamentally different in their cultural identities, which are reflected in virtually every aspect of college life (AIHEC & IHEP, 1999; Stein, 1992). The mission of TCUs is not to "mimic mainstream institutions but to reflect and sustain a unique tribal identity" (Boyer, 2002, p. 18). Despite their unique mission and identity, and the significant progress they have made the last few decades, TCUs remain largely unknown outside of Indian country (Guillory & Ward, 2008). For mainstream student affairs professionals who may be unfamiliar with TCUs, the question is, what are the benefits of collaborating with a TCU?

Benefits of Collaboration

TCUs and mainstream university collaborations have several benefits, including sharing resources, increased access, sharing best practices for Native student success, and increased research opportunities. Following are examples of these benefits.

Shared Resources

Sharing lies at the heart of collaboration. Sharing resources, information, ideas, and knowledge is one of the many benefits of collaboration. As Nichols, Baird, and Kayongo-Male (2001) observe, "Many institutions are drawn to partnerships as a means of expanding their access to resources such as funding, facilities, academic expertise and cultural insights" (p. 20). TCUs have cultural knowledge and expertise, but they often lack physical resources, such as equipment, buildings, and space, that mainstream institutions may have. One of the benefits of collaboration is the ability to position the institutions to pursue competitive grant opportunities and develop joint projects to increase the chances of winning funding for grant proposals that can enhance the academic, student, or organizational programming efforts at each institution. Both institutions benefit through capacity-building efforts via shared resources.

Increased Access

TCUs were designed to provide Native students access and pathways to higher education. Since many TCUs are located in remote areas, they are often the *only* option for higher education. From this perspective, access to higher education is not something to be taken for granted but an opportunity to improve one's way of life and future (AIHEC & IHEP, 1999). Many Native students enter TCUs with the intention of transferring to mainstream institutions upon degree completion. This presents a tremendous opportunity for tribal and nontribal institutions to develop collaborative partnerships to provide degree pathways for Native students while minimizing barriers such as geographic location. Although the steady increase in TCU enroll-ment is promising, access and success remain issues for Native students (Akweks, Bill, Seppanen, & Smith, 2009). Academic success is still the exception rather than the norm, and increased access is only part of the solution. Innovative collaborations are one way institutions can further expand Native students' access to higher education to ensure that they have the necessary support and resources to succeed at their institution of choice.

Best Practices for Native Student Success

Research indicates that Native students are more likely to earn a four-year degree at mainstream institutions after first attending a tribal college (Ameri-can Indian College Fund [AICF], 2003; Ortiz & HeavyRunner, 2003). This is significant given that tribal colleges draw students who often view educa-tional systems with mistrust. The typical tribal college student is a first-generation, Pell Grant–eligible, single mother in her 30s with limited college readiness skills (AIHEC & IHEP, 1999). What can mainstream institutions learn by collaborating with TCUs to retain and graduate all Native students? Perhaps it is unrealistic, if not untenable, to expect mainstream institutions to engage fully in the kind of student and cultural programming TCUs are uniquely qualified to undertake. However, TCUs rely on some best practices to improve the academic performance of Native students (Boyer, 1997), such as emphasizing strong connections to family, community, and cultural iden-tity (HeavyRunner & Marshall, 2003; Ortiz & HeavyRunner, 2003; Water-man, 2007). Not every mainstream institution is able to implement these approaches fully for various reasons; however, collaboration can be the vehi-cle through which tribal and nontribal institutions discuss best practices for Native student success and learn from one another how to retain and gradu-ate Native students.

Increased Research Opportunities

Although TCUs did not start out as research institutions, the potential for them to engage in graduate or undergraduate research emerged when they received land-grant status in 1994 (Gayton-Swisher, 2004). TCUs are contin-ually building their capacity to support scholarship and research by develop-ing libraries, tribal archives, and other essential resources to support research activities (Tippeconnic & McKinney, 2003). Increased research capacity also means increased collaboration opportunities, particularly with research uni-versities. University research faculty can partner with TCU faculty to provide professional development and training opportunities. Furthermore, collaborations can benefit university researchers by involving them in joint research projects that directly benefit tribal communities, increase scholarly understanding of Native American issues, introduce and incorporate culturally relevant research models, build trusting relationships to support community-based research and community service projects, and provide opportunities to interact with and involve undergraduate tribal college students in projects that may lead to increased Native student recruitment and retention at mainstream universities (Johnson, Bartgis, Worley, Hellman, & Burkhart, 2010).

Examples of Collaborative Partnerships

Nichols and Monette (2003) highlight several successful tribal and mainstream collaborations as part of the Native American Higher Education Initiative (NAHEI), funded by the W.K. Kellogg Foundation. One collaboration, between Sinte Gleska University (SGU) and the University of California–Los Angeles (UCLA), used a community-based approach to integrate academic and artistic program delivery in Native theater. Results of the Culture Matters: Project HOOP (Honoring Our Origins and People) project included

- the development and delivery of eight new theater courses at SGU;
- new course materials, such as the *Stories of Our Ways* anthology and *American Indian Theater in Performance: A Reader*, created and published by the UCLA American Indian Studies Center;
- a 100% retention rate of first-year theater students; and
- a video on diabetes awareness, produced in collaboration with local Indian Health Service personnel as a teaching tool for community members.

Another collaboration among Leech Lake Tribal College, SGU, and Bemidji State University (BSU), called Students Matter, focused on increasing enrollment and improving retention at Leech Lake Tribal College and BSU by using distance-learning technology (e.g., interactive TV and online courses) to allow students to complete four-year degrees at the Leech Lake campus site. Preliminary results of the Students Matter project include

- upper-level elementary education courses, which local tribal leaders identified as a critical need on the Leech Lake Ojibwa reservation

offered at Leech Lake Tribal College through an agreement with
SGU;

- access to BSU's distance-learning degree programs by Leech Lake
  Tribal College students;
- a 38% increase in BSU's American Indian student enrollment, from
  142 in 1996–1997 to 197 in 1999–2000; a 200% enrollment increase
  of Leech Lake Tribal College students at BSU in 1998–1999; and a
  300% increase in the number of Native students earning four-year
  degrees; and
- a Native retention counselor position created at BSU, resulting in a
  50% decrease in early withdrawals and increased retention of Native
  students.

Collaborations can also involve multiple institutions working together
to affect educational policy at the state level, such as the Partnership for
Native American College Access and Success, cofunded by the Lumina Foundation and the Bill and Melinda Gates Foundation. This multi-institutional
collaboration in Washington State includes two tribal and three nontribal
colleges—Northwest Indian College, the Evergreen State College, Antioch
University–Seattle, Muckleshoot Tribal College, and Grays Harbor College,
which together compiled the comprehensive *Pathways Report* on Indian education efforts at the postsecondary level. Authored by representatives from
these institutions and the Washington Board of Technical and Community
Colleges, the report contains extensive Native education profiles of nearly all
colleges and universities in Washington State. It also includes strategies to
foster collaborations among higher education institutions, tribes, and stakeholders (Akweks et al., 2009).

Land-grant institutions are another vehicle for TCU collaborations.
Montana, for example, has seven TCUs and a public land-grant institution
(Montana State University), whose common interest to advance their land-
grant missions resulted in the creation of the American Indian Research
Opportunities (AIRO) programs, which address the serious underrepresentation of American Indians in biomedical/health sciences. Designed to
encourage Native students to pursue careers in medicine or science, AIRO
programming has expanded to all areas of science, math, engineering, and
technology ("Collaborations flourish . . . ," 2002). Institutional leaders
reported that these types of collaborations, "not only help the institutions
fulfill their land grant missions, but they offer cultural and financial benefits
to all" (p. 1). These examples demonstrate the variety and potential impact

of successful collaborations. Of course, collaborations may offer as many challenges as they do benefits. The following are examples of some of the barriers to successful collaborations.

Barriers to Collaboration

There is a degree of cautiousness on the part of TCU leaders when it comes to collaborating with mainstream institutions. When TCUs were established, many were "ignored at first, or even deliberately shunned" by their mainstream counterparts (Boyer, 1995, p. 13). Furthermore, when TCUs started showing signs of growth and success, many of these same mainstream institutions started duplicating TCU programs. This practice of co-opting has left a bad taste in the mouths of many TCU leaders, especially when TCU courses of similar content to mainstream course offerings were not approved for transfer credit.

TCUs can also be an attractive partner for the wrong reasons. Mainstream institutions may initiate partnerships with TCUs for the sole purpose of securing grants or other types of funding sources with little to no regard for equity in finances, decision making, authority, or other matters (Nichols & Monette, 2003). Boyer (1995) notes that some mainstream institutions regularly collaborated with TCUs on grant projects but "took a disproportionate share of the money or did not deliver the promised goods" (p. 14). Institutions that initiate partnerships with TCUs motivated by self-interest only perpetuate the lack of trust undermining the benefits of genuine collaborations and underscore why many TCU leaders maintain a cautious collaborator persona when it comes to collaborations involving funding.

Perhaps one of the most subtle and dangerous barriers to TCU collaborations is the perception that TCUs are not as academically rigorous as or are of lesser quality than nontribal institutions. This negative perception can be traced back to the beginning of the tribal college movement when many people believed Indians could not run a college, let alone a quality college (Stein, 1992). In fact, TCUs are fully accredited institutions that are required to meet the same academic standards as all other accredited colleges and universities (AICF, 2010). Negative perceptions or assumptions can hamper any collaboration, especially if one partner believes it is superior to the other. In contrast, when both partners view themselves as equals, they relate and communicate to each other as if they are on a level playing field and are more likely to bring out the best in each other and create a successful partnership.

It is well known among tribes that nontribal university researchers have historically engaged in research on tribal populations to advance their own careers, often at the expense of the tribes they studied, resulting in the exploitation and stereotyping of tribal people (Christopher, Knows His Gun-McCormick, Young, & Watts, 2008). As a result, many tribes and TCUs have taken measures to gain more control over research projects by establishing their own institutional review boards to prevent exploitive practices and ensure that research directly benefits their people and is conducted in a culturally appropriate and respectful manner (Crazy Bull, 1997; Hernandez, 2004; Noley, 1993). The silver lining in this sullied history involving research is that future collaborations between mainstream institutions and TCUs can learn from the lessons of the past and engage in joint research projects the right way, in the true spirit of collaboration and goodwill. Such projects should move away from viewing Natives as a population to be "researched" to seeing the population as an equal partner in all aspects of the project.

Recommendations to Practitioners and/or Institutions

In light of the benefits and challenges of collaborations, the following recommendations are offered for developing TCU and mainstream institution collaborations. These recommendations are not intended to be exhaustive but rather practical guidelines for consideration. First, determine the appropriate fit. Building partnerships is a process, not a program (Martin, 2004). Part of the initial process is to determine whether there are common interests to build on. Questions to ask include: Does this partnership align with the institutional mission, priorities, and academic programs? Does each institution have the capacity required, or will this lead to capacity building? Can the partnership be sustained? One way for institutions to determine the appropriate fit is to showcase relevant information, such as strategic plans, degree programs, initiatives, and relevant data, so each partner has an opportunity to learn about the other's institutional history, priorities, programming, and the like. This will go a long way in identifying potential institutional alignments as well as gaps and weaknesses.

Second, recognize that tribal colleges, like the tribes they reflect, are unique. Developing a relationship with a tribal college means developing a relationship with an individual tribe. Each tribe has its own distinct history, culture, and language; consequently, success with one tribal college may not be achieved with another. Each partnership must be developed on its own terms. Be sure to put everything in writing. It is strongly recommended that institutions enter into formal contractual agreements, such as articulation agreements or memorandums of agreement/understanding. These formal agreements explicitly outline the expectations and responsibility of each institution. In addition, these agreements should be signed by the president or another high-level administrator at each institution to ensure that the partnership has backing and support at the highest level.

Third, develop clear communication roles and channels. It goes without saying that communication is at the heart of all agreements and partnerships. What does clear communication involve? Are face-to-face meetings preferred? How often and when? How are decisions made, by whom, and when? What is the decision-making process? How is information shared and disseminated? Questions like these need to be taken into consideration to avoid generalizations and assumptions and to minimize misunderstandings.

Fourth, remain flexible. Collaborations are fluid; plans and people change. Institutions that are adept at adjusting to changes in plans, personnel, priorities, or economic conditions are those likely to sustain long-term partnerships. This includes flexibility and openness to cultural protocols, commonalities, and differences.

Fifth, take time to build trust. Building and maintaining trust is an ongoing process (Christopher et al., 2008). Trust can be built on many levels by acknowledging one another's expertise; listening as much as, if not more than, talking during group meetings; respecting each other's ideas and contributions; matching actions to words; being honest and sincere without any hidden motives; and being respectful and considerate (Christopher et al., 2008). When trust and respect are present, participants feel free to bring their gifts and talents to the process and express their ideas openly without fear of being judged or ignored.

Sixth, choose the right personnel. Whether a university tribal liaison, faculty member, or tribal college administrator, these individuals should serve as the single point of contact between each institution. Often, the difference between good or bad collaborations may hinge on the right person. This individual is a reflection of the partnering institution. Nichols et al. (2001) found that valuable individual characteristics included cross-cultural competence, open-mindedness, willingness to listen, flexibility, commitment, patience, persistence, and honesty. Therefore, these individuals need to possess not only the right skill set and attitude but also the willingness and follow-through to be accountable to the partnership.

Seventh, keep students a priority. It is easy to lose sight of students when we get involved in the minutia of relationship building, but perhaps the most important question that needs to be asked is: How is this partnership or collaboration going to enhance student learning? For example, it is common for Native people to think seven generations ahead when making key decisions that will affect the tribe as a whole (Deloria, 1991). In this case, TCU leaders should ask themselves, how will this decision or partnership affect our people seven generations from now? Asking student-centered questions like this will ensure that collaborations and outcomes are mindful of students' needs and interests for years to come.

Conclusion

The purpose of this chapter is to provide practical strategies and considerations for mainstream professionals who are interested in collaborating or planning to collaborate with a TCU. As institutions across America face downsizing as a result of the harsh economic climate, the need for partnerships led by courageous leadership and optimism will grow. In higher education, teaching and learning are not limited to the classroom. Opportunities for teaching and learning between institutions abound, and this is certainly the case between tribal and mainstream institutions if done in a mutually respectful and equitable way. One lesson learned from collaborations is that the best are those in which each institution emerges stronger as a result—academically, financially, organizationally, and/or relationally. Institutions will certainly need to be stronger to persist through the financial, social, educational, and cultural challenges that lie ahead. This is one path that Native people, and TCUs, know all too well.

References

Akweks, K., Bill, N., Seppanen L., & Smith, B. L. (2009). Pathways for Native American students: A report on colleges and universities in Washington. A report from the Partnership for Native American College Access & Success project. Retrieved March 16, 2012, from http://www.evergreen.edu/nativeprograms/conferencesandreports.htm

American Indian College Fund (AICF). (2003). *Cultivating success: The critical value of American Indian scholarships and the positive impact of tribal college capital construction.* Retrieved October 1, 2010, from http://www.collegefund.org/userfiles/file/CultivatingSuccess.pdf

American Indian College Fund (AICF). (2010). *Tribal colleges.* Retrieved October 1, 2010, from http://www.collegefund.org/content/tribal_colleges

American Indian Higher Education Consortium (AIHEC) & Institute for Higher Education Policy (IHEP). (1999). Tribal colleges: An introduction. Washington DC: Authors. Retrieved July 26, 2010, from http://www.aihec.org/resources/archives.cfm

Boyer, P. (1995). Tomorrow's tribal college will redefine the culture of its tribe, and help shape national policy. *Tribal College Journal, 7*(1), 8.

Boyer, P. (1997). *Native American colleges: Progress and prospects.* Princeton, NJ: Princeton University Press.

Boyer, P. (2002). Defying the odds: Tribal colleges conquer skepticism but still face persistent challenges. *Tribal College Journal, 14*(2), 12–18.

Christopher, S., Knows His Gun-McCormick, A., Young, S., & Watts, V. (2008). Building and maintaining trust in a community-based participatory research partnership. *American Journal of Public Health, 98*(8), 1398–1407.

Collaborations flourish between MSU, tribal colleges. (2002, December 25). *Indian Country Today*, pp. 0–C1. Retrieved from http://search.proquest.com/docview/362724694?accountid=13567

Crazy Bull, C. (1997). A Native conversation about research and scholarship. *Tribal College Journal, 8*(17), 17–23.

Crazy Bull, C. (2009). Tribal college and universities: From where we are to where we might go. In L. S. Warner & G. E. Gipp (Eds.), *Tradition and culture in the millennium: Tribal colleges and universities* (pp. 209–217). Charlotte, NC: Information Age.

Deloria, V., Jr. (1991). *Indian education in America: 8 essays by Vine Deloria, Jr.* Boulder, CO: American Indian Science & Engineering Society.

Gayton-Swisher, K. (2004). Pursuing their potential: TCUs turn from being researched to being researchers. *Tribal College Journal, 16*(2), 8–10.

Guillory, J. P., & Ward, K. (2008). Tribal colleges and universities: Identity, invisibility, and current issues. In M. Gasman, B. Baez, & C. S. V. Turner (Eds.), *Understanding minority-serving institutions* (pp. 91–110). Albany, NY: SUNY Press.

HeavyRunner, I., & Marshall, K. (2003). 'Miracle survivors': Promoting resilience in Indian students. *Tribal College Journal, 14*(4), 14–18.

Hernandez, J. A. A. (2004). Blood, lies, and Indian rights: TCUs becoming gatekeepers for research. *Tribal College Journal, 16*(2), 10–13.

Horse, P. G. (2005). Native American Identity. In M. J. T. Fox, S. C. Lowe, & G. S. McClellen (Eds.), *Serving Native American students* (pp. 61–68). San Francisco: Jossey-Bass.

Johnson, C. V., Bartgis, J., Worley, J. A., Hellman, C. M., & Burkhart, R. (2010). Urban Indian voices: A community-based participatory research health and needs assessment. *American Indian and Alaska Native Mental Health Research Journal, 17*(1), 49–71.

Lomawaima, K. T. (1999). The unnatural history of American Indian education. In K. G. Swisher & J. W. Tippeconnic III (Eds.), *Next steps: Research and practice to advance Indian education* (pp. 1–31). Charleston, WV: AEL, Inc.

Lomawaima, K. T., & McCarty, T. L. (2002). When tribal sovereignty challenges democracy: American Indian education and the democratic ideal. *American Education Research Journal, 39,* 279–306.

Martin, J. (2004). *Building a strategic partnership is a process, not a program.* Paper presented at the University of Montana American Council of Education Conference, "A Summit for Native American Faculty and Administrators in Higher Education," April 24–26, 2004, Missoula, MT.

Nichols, T., J., Baird, P., & Kayongo-Male, D. (2001). Partnerships offer promise and perils: A study of collaborations with state universities. *Tribal College Journal, 13*(2), 20–23.

Nichols, T. J., & Kayongo-Male, D. M. (2003). The dynamics of tribal college–state university collaboration. *Journal of American Indian Education, 42,* 1–24.

Nichols, T., & Monette, G. (2003). Linking tribal colleges and mainstream institutions: Fundamental tensions and lessons learned. In M. K. P. Benham & W. J. Stein (Eds.), *The renaissance of American Indian higher education: Capturing the dream* (pp. 121–135). Mahwah, NJ: Lawrence Erlbaum.

Noley, G. (1993). Finding answers to old questions: By working together, universities and tribal colleges can meet the research needs of American Indian communities. *Tribal College Journal, 4*(4), 24.

Ortiz, A. M., & HeavyRunner, I. (2003). Student access, retention, and success: Models of inclusion and support. In M. K. P. Benham & W. J. Stein (Eds.), *The renaissance of American Indian higher education: Capturing the dream* (pp. 215–240). Mahwah, NJ: Lawrence Erlbaum.

Stein, W. J. (1992). *Tribally controlled colleges: Making good medicine.* New York: Peter Lang.

Stein, W. J. (2009). Tribal colleges and universities: Supporting the revitalization in Indian country. In L. S. Warner & G. E. Gipp (Eds.), *Tradition and culture in the millennium: Tribal colleges and universities* (pp. 17–34). Charlotte, NC: Information Age.

Tippeconnic, J. W., III, & McKinney, S. (2003). Native faculty: Scholarship and development. In M. K. P. Benham & W. J. Stein (Eds.), *The renaissance of American Indian higher education: Capturing the dream* (pp. 241–255). Mahwah, NJ: Lawrence Erlbaum.

Waterman, S. J. (2007). A complex path to Haudenosaunee degree completion. *Journal of American Indian Education, 46*(1), 20–40.

7

ACADEMIC AND STUDENT AFFAIRS PARTNERSHIPS

Native American Student Affairs Units

Molly Springer (Cherokee Nation of Oklahoma), Dr. Charlotte E. Davidson (Diné/Mandan, Hidatsa, and Arikara), and Dr. Stephanie J. Waterman (Onondaga, Turtle)

The counterpart to Native American Studies programs (NAS), academic units concerning the study of Native America, are the Native American/American Indian student affairs units. Champagne and Stauss (2002) have written *the* book regarding NAS units. However, the history and development of the student side—student affairs units/services—is directly connected to NAS programs, as most of these are charged with supporting students (Champagne & Stauss, 2002). Because Native American student affairs is a relatively new field, often associated with an academic unit or multicultural office, the authors chose Native American Student Services Unit (NASSU) as a general label simply for this discussion. Whereas Western hierarchies characteristically promote inequality, top-down control, and individualism, and are linear and masculine in orientation, an Indigenous "way of being" is circular and balanced—a paradigm imbued with a spiritual language that promotes harmony, healing, kinship, and masculine and feminine balance, and that is ecologically oriented (Emerson, 2002, as cited by McAlpin, 2008). Given the differences in orientation, how do NASSUs function within Western-oriented non-Native colleges and universities (NNCUs)?

"[E]ducational institutions are sites that can be used in the coordination, creation, and practices of Indigenous projects" (McAlpin, 2008, p. 115). One

of the primary steps toward decolonization, in the context of higher education, is reinvesting the community with control over educational processes
to create an empowering university context for students (Smith, 1999). This
type of work can be seen on many campuses where the presence of culturally
unique spaces and Native-centered programming has allowed for the building of a "new" narrative into institutions of higher education (Williams &
Tanaka, 2007). This chapter addresses the strengths in certain NASSU programs, provides a short history of the NASSU and its unique characteristics,
and looks at three successful model units. Because this book is intended as a
resource for staff at NNCUs, we do not discuss tribal colleges. We urge a
dedicated look at student affairs systems within tribal colleges and universities (TCUs).

Ethnic and Multicultural Student Support Centers

While this chapter is about NASSU, we begin with a short review of the
development of ethnic support centers. All multicultural student support
offices and cultural centers are the result of the Civil Rights Era (Patton,
2005). Rojas (2007) argues that Black studies was a direct result of the Black
Power movement. Civil unrest, demands for equality, and President Lyndon
Johnson's War on Poverty resulted in numbers of students of color attending
college as never before. Passage of the 1965 Higher Education Act (HEA)
increased financial aid, opening the doors for students of color. As a result
of the 1965 HEA, a college could access funds for the underprivileged. Federal [TRIO] Programs were developed that focused on college "talent"
search, college preparation, and student support, although it should be noted
that these programs did not serve tribal colleges until 1990 (U.S. Congress,
1998). Furthermore, these programs (Veterans Upward Bound, Upward
Bound Math-Science, Upward Bound, TRIO Student Support Services, and
the Ronald E. McNair Postbaccalaureate Achievement Program) are housed
within host institutions to increase degree attainment across various fields of
study up to the postgraduate level.[1] The missions of these programs were
fulfilled mainly by serving thousands of African American students. However, as Patton and Hannon (2008) write,

> Despite the swelling Black enrollment at these institutions, campus admin-
> istrators had done very little to prepare for the arrival of these students . . .
> these students were expected to assimilate were . . . plagued by racism,
> oppression, and discrimination. Unwilling to assimilate or forfeit their own

cultural values and identity, African American students and their allies began to protest and conduct sit-ins, demanding that PWIs [predominantly White institutions] . . . provide offices and facilities where they could meet and commune in a safe, non hostile environment. (p. 142)

In response, Indiana University's Black House was created in 1969 as the first such center to aid in efforts to retain African American students on campus. At the time, Native students were also expected to assimilate to the college campus, a similar sink-or-swim proposition.

History of the Native American Student Support Unit

The rationale for NASSU was largely in response to a lack of support on campus for Native students, even though other ethnic or multicultural support units had been established. NAS and NASSU were created out of both student and community persistence (Champagne & Stauss, 2002). For example, at Cornell University, the American Indian Program (AIP) was the result of the recommendation of a committee of staff, faculty, and students "to serve Indian students and expand interest in Indian affairs on campus" (Unser, 2001, p. 36), and to expand outreach to the community. The committee, the driving force in establishing AIP at Cornell, emphasized student services as well as Native studies from the beginning (http://aip.cornell.edu). NAS programs have been criticized for being "geared primarily toward student services" (Champagne & Stauss, 2002, p. 11); consequently, NASSU is often dependent on the collaboration and strength of the NAS program on campus.

As indicated in the introduction to this book, Native Americans are greatly outnumbered on college campuses, which means we need each other to survive. Because of this overarching need, students, staff, and faculty cross academic barriers, class, and power structures to connect, and through these critical connections, they build structures of support in a collaborative way. The newly established Payne Family Native American Center is an example of such a center that crosses academic borders, combining NAS and NASSU in one central space.

[I]ntentionally designed to serve as the home for academic support services and provide an intellectual and social hub for all those interested in learning about Native American history, issues, culture, and perspectives and a center that would include: collaborating among the diverse Native American educational programs across the campus; provide a space for students to gather, to assist in the transition to life on campus; to explore the intersections between the traditions of Native American and non-Native American cultures, and "provide an epicenter" for tribal leaders across Montana and beyond to gather, join forces, and tackle some of the most pressing issues they share. (University of Montana Native American Center, 2012, p. 2)

Placement of the Native American Student Support Unit

The placement of NASSU is shaped by campus history and by an administration's Native American knowledge base. Like many ethnic programs, a NASSU can find itself in a rather marginalized area on campus, inhibiting growth and hampering visibility (Patton, 2005). It is important to note that this placement is not usually intentional, but the result of a combination of a lack of knowledge about the good and intentional work of Native American student affairs as a field, and a general lack of literature and knowledge regarding Native American education by both student affairs administrators and faculty (Champagne & Stauss, 2002).

Most NASSUs were simply established under the framework of diversity units already on a campus. For example, if a multicultural center was in place, a Native American piece was placed within it, rarely with any research on what might be the *right* placement for its growth and security. NAS faculty can and have advocated for where NASSUs should be placed. However, because faculty rarely have a student affairs or student development education, even their input can be given without knowledge of student affairs. While closely linked, NAS is different from Native American student affairs. As academic units, NAS must fulfill academic demands first, answering to academic affairs officers and the requirements of their academic discipline.

Inserting a NASSU into a blended or "*multi*cultural" space can further marginalize Native American students. Native American students live on land that was colonized by the very institutions from which they seek an education. Treaties and other policy agreements, laws, and Native American sovereignty are part of our students' experiences. No other population comes to college with these characteristics. There is also the vast diversity of Native America, which includes over 500 federally recognized tribal nations (Wilkins, 2002). A "best practices" model of placement does not exist. What we do know is that students flourish when they have a structure that fosters intentional challenge and support (Sanford, 1962), offers assistance with navigation and involvement, and offers a "home away from home" that encourages retention (Astin, 1993; Shotton, Yellowfish, & Cintrón, 2010).

Ideally, an autonomous unit is best for the stability of any multicultural/ethnic support unit (Patton, 2005). If a NASSU is to be successful, and build a program that relies on the cultural interests and needs of the students it serves, the surrounding community, and the institutional mission, a cookie cutter mold will not suffice. Collaborations with multiple partners in both student affairs and academic affairs are an essential tool in building a program that can move toward self-determination and growth, and can have the support and stamina to stand on its own.

Programming for the Native American Student Support Unit

A Native student on campus can have multiple academic, financial, social, and cultural problems. In fact, because a NASSU is small and often understaffed, campus networks must be extensive to provide the necessary connections for Native students. The numerical comparison to other groups remarginalizes the potential of such a unit. The NASSU must be in communication with the other commonly used campus units and act as a liaison to those units, even though NASSUs are typically not well funded or well staffed because of the low number of Native students on campus. Yet, the needs of our students are far-reaching, which is true of other multicultural/ethnic units as well (Patton, 2005). For example, Harvard University's Native American Program (HUNAP) promotes learning communities. HUNAP hosts a colloquia series in which students, faculty, and staff come together to share and expand upon scholarly topics, while hosting year-round academic, cultural, and social events for its students. Further examples of programming are in the models at the end of this chapter.

NASSU programming and structure is typically defined externally by other communities on campus because the unit is subject to the needs of the division in which it is housed as a whole. For example, when a unit is within a student affairs division, it would be expected to assess Native student programming in the same way as other student affairs divisions. If housed within an academic affairs unit (such as NAS), the NASSU may have a different means of assessment directed by academic affairs.

Director of the Native American Student Support Unit

The head of any NASSU is a very complex and demanding position. The director must contend with the lack of understanding among university administrators on the subject of "Indianness" and ethnic matters in Native America (Champagne & Stauss, 2002; Pewewardy & Frey, 2004). University administrators often do not understand the fundamental facts about American Indians and generally classify them as a small ethnic group. Issues of Tribal membership and federally recognized Tribes and their rights are little understood by and complicate the task of university administration. (Champagne & Stauss, 2002, p. 6)

This includes the student affairs side of campus.

NASSU directors must wear different hats and fill various roles for their students and campus community. The NASSU director often coordinates the following, with or without a staff: visit the hospital when a student is sick; visit with parents and family when they are in town; advocate for students with faculty advisors who have no knowledge, stereotyped knowledge, or little knowledge of Native Americans; advocate with scholarship and financial aid departments and encourage creative thinking on policy; help the registrar's office understand tribal deadlines, which vary according to tribe; work with student organizations to learn about Native student needs and understand that only 10, *yes, only 10*, students can, and do, organize the biggest campus event of the year—the annual pow-wow; and advocate to campus security that the drum "noise" is a sacred cultural piece of the students' well-being, and students should not need to get a permit every time they pull out their drums. The director helps our student body develop political sophistication, such as understanding the difference between Native feminism and non-Native feminism, while still partnering with the women's center/studies. NASSU directors are expected to gather Native students for "multicultural" gatherings to be visible on campus; dispel misconceptions that TRIO programs fulfill all of our needs; and guard against exploiting Native students in committee work, recruitment, and campus image. The unit may also conduct academic advisement because our students often trust a Native person's opinion over the opinion of someone with initials after his or her name. Considering the assimilationist intent of Native American education in this country (see this book's introduction; Carney, 1999), it is no wonder that these units fulfill myriad roles. In addition, the director must have the blessing of the Native community and have the *skills* to do the work. Of course, having a Native American student affairs specialist who can also be the recruiter, counselor, administrator, community builder, and sole grant writer is like winning the 50/50 raffle at a pow-wow—where, much like drawing the winning ticket, it is a lottery governed by good fortune and a lot of luck. This is especially true when there are so few Native American student affairs specialists—Native and non-Native, in graduate programs or working in the field.

Funding of the Native American Student Support Unit

As it is for other support units, funding is a challenge. With the majority of people on campus unaware of our students, or when they exist only as "an asterisk" in a report (Garland, 2007), it can be difficult to be awarded the necessary budget. Yet, looking to others for building resources for your community is not very self-determinate. So how do we gain funding?

Funding for NASSUs is found through a number of different vehicles. There are collaborative efforts of multiple communities and departments to jointly support programming, private and alumni donations, fund-raising sales, scholarship drives, corporate and small-business grants, not-for-profit grants, and endowments. Dartmouth College is the only model of its kind in the country with an endowment. This external endowment comes through the student affairs operating budget. Its history of supporting Native students for 40 years is unparalleled; Dartmouth's endowment allows for its independence.

Resources typically are based on quantitative and numerical data and assessment. Other campus groups and administration often view student numbers as the determining factor for resources. Champagne and Stauss (2002) state that NAS programs are "often small . . . ad hoc organizations . . . in danger of incorporation into other disciplines or into ethnic or American Studies programs" (p. 11). The same issue of being a "small" unit within a unit that may be struggling itself to survive puts NASSUs in danger of being incorporated into a blended space, such as a multicultural or ethnic student support center. Yet, just because student numbers are smaller than other populations does not mean our work is any less valuable. See our NASSU models for more examples of funding.

Why Native American Student Support Units Matter

Native American cultural houses and centers support students' personal, cultural, and academic growth (McAlpin, 2008; Shotton et al., 2010), and also serve as resource hubs to welcome and celebrate the uniqueness of our students. Not to be diminished is the manner in which these centers endeavor to design programming that advances the self-determinate needs of the local Native community, as well as those of tribal nations to which students belong. Working in accord with various departmental units on college campuses is critical to achieving the shared vision of graduating students from the tertiary level of their education. An array of multifaceted support systems currently exists as a means to enrich what could be an otherwise impersonal educational experience for Native students. For example, the Stanford University American Indian, Alaska Native and Native Hawaiian Program (AIANNHP)/Native American Cultural Center (NACC, n.d.) is one of the stellar programs in the country. Its online literature details the historicity of Muwekma-Tah-Ruk (the center's Native-themed house), and provides an inner picture of who it is and what it does concerning recruitment, orientation, advisement, counseling, student organizations, monthly and annual programs, and intralibrary loans. The question, "why do we exist?" is answered in AIANNHP and NACC's mission statement, where they posit their overall goal to nurture students throughout their journeyed accession through the academic pipeline, as being mediated through a team of staff members who possess practical, cultural, and institutional understandings of best student development practices (NACC, n.d.).

While a multitude of programming is provided through the University of North Dakota's American Indian Student Services (AISS) (Brown, 2005), a unique aspect of its support is illustrated through the university's policy of burning cedar, sweetgrass, and sage. Citing the 1978 American Indian/Alaska Native Religious Freedom Act, Native students are guaranteed the right to use cedar, sweetgrass, and sage within campus housing and nonclassroom buildings for ceremonial purposes.[2] What can be gleaned from this policy is the necessity and importance of spiritual sustainability within the realm of academia. Integral to maintaining balance and the processes of academic, cultural, and personal growth of students (McAlpin, 2008), spiritual rootedness should be perceived as a means to aid students in renewing efficacy and cultural values.

Native American Student Support Unit Models

Following are three NASSU models as examples of their diversity. The reader should note that these student support centers are the result of grassroots movements. Websites for additional information are found at the end of this chapter.

Portland State University: Native American Student Services and Native American Student Community Center [3]

A truly collaborative effort by Native American/Alaskan Native students and alumni, Portland State University administrators, the Tribes of Oregon, and Portland-area Native American communities produced the Native American

Student and Community Center (NASCC) with a commitment to serve the multiple constituencies supportive of the vision and the creation of the facility (NASCC, 2012). A "cultural home" for Native American, Alaska Native, and Pacific Islander students, the center has a classroom where NAS classes are taught, a large gathering space, meeting rooms, a computer lab open to students and the public, a kitchen, the office of the coordinator of Native American Student Services, and an office shared by three student clubs—UISHE (United Indian Students in Higher Education, founded in the late 1970s), a chapter of AISES (the American Indian Science and Engineering Society), and PIC (Pacific Islander Club). Student groups, the campus community, local Native American organizations, and the tribes all use the center, which hosts an Honor Day Graduation Ceremony—a capstone event common among NASSUs across the country.

The mutual efforts of Native American students and alumni, the university, the tribes of Oregon, the metro Native American communities, and private donors and foundations culminated in the construction of the NASCC, or in their words, "a home away from home" for Native American, Alaska Native, and Pacific Islander students. Day-to-day operations are managed by the NASCC specialist and trained student assistants, most of whom are Native or Alaska Native. Outreach and academic support services are the responsibility of the coordinator of Native American Student Services, a position created in 1992—the first position on campus to serve a specific ethnic population. Both positions report to the executive director of Diversity and Multicultural Student Services (DMSS), under the vice president for Enrollment Management and Student Affairs. The DMSS department includes three TRIO programs; two additional coordinators (for Latina/o students and African American students); the multicultural center; and La Casa Latina, a new Latino Student Support Center created in June 2011. Funding to support the center's operations comes from institutional funds and leasing fees; the center is a "mock" auxiliary. Very recently, student incidental fees were allocated to support the center's student programs.

Most notable, the center has an advisory board comprising students, faculty, staff, local Native American community representatives, and a tribal representative, along with two seats for civic leaders (NASCC, 2011). The role of this board is to provide advisement to the executive director of DMSS and the center's staff to ensure that the NASCC's short- and long-term goals are fulfilled and rooted in Indigenous cultural mores. The advisory board also takes an active role in fund-raising for scholarships and programming.

Cornell University: American Indian Program and Akwe:kon

As an example of the intimate linking of student support with NAS, we present a short history of Cornell's AIP. In the 1970s Frank Bonamie, a Cayuga chief, was convinced that Native student attrition was the fault of the institution and not student ability. An ad hoc committee was formed to analyze the problem, as referred to in chapter 3. The committee recommended hiring a graduate student to recruit Native students and to develop policies and practices to improve retention. In 1975 the first American Indian studies (AIS) faculty member was hired. The program grew, and its director, Ronald LaFrance (Mohawk), initiated the concept and building of Akwe:kon (the Native student house), increased new staff lines and outreach, and oversaw the academic expansion of AIP. Still setting the tone of this vision is AIP's aim of developing and educating new generations that will "contemplate, study and contribute to the building of Nation and community in America" (http://aip.cornell.edu). Staffing includes a director, an associate director, a student development specialist, a residence hall director, a faculty affiliate, an administrative assistant, and student employees. The AIP structural makeup involves its director reporting to the College of Agriculture and Life Sciences, whereas Akwe:kon (a residential house) is jointly supported by AIP and Campus Life. Sitting in the heart of Haudenosaunee (Iroquois) territory, Akwe:kon features Haudenosaunee symbols and colors. AIP is supported through funds from Cornell University's Office of the Provost, Cornell's College of Agriculture and Life Sciences, and the Office of the Dean, while scholarship and outreach funds are furnished by individual donors.

Purdue University: Native American Educational and Cultural Center

Like its northwest and northeastern NASSU counterparts, the emergence of the Native American Educational and Cultural Center (NAECC) was initiated primarily by Native American students, along with members of the campus community, both of whom resolutely expressed a need for a campus space for Native students. This movement, otherwise known as the Tecumseh Project (a grassroots initiative that assisted postgraduate students with research projects), aided in the eventual birth of NAECC (NAECC, 2011b). Under the auspices of the Division of Diversity and Inclusion (DDI), NAECC's primary aim is to encourage a Native-centered learning community for an intertribal constituency of Native American, Alaska Native, and

Native Hawaiian students. Fully funded with the institutional commitment of the Office of the Provost and DDI, the NAECC merits attention for the additional support it receives from the National Science Foundation (NSF), the Sloan Indigenous Graduate Program, and ADVANCE Purdue, all of which help NAECC's retention and recruitment efforts. The NAECC aligns the viewpoint of its mission with Purdue's three campus initiatives of "Launching Tomorrow's Leaders," "Discovery with Delivery," and "Meeting Global Challenges" by placing an organizational premium on (a) yielding a successive generation of degree-bearing Native scholars who can promote issues in their home communities; (b) generating support for research and scholarship funding, as it pertains to Native American people; and (c) cultivating non-Native appreciation of the plural contexts of Indigenous Peoples (NAECC, 2011a). Staffing includes a director, administrative assistant, and part-time student position, and its space includes a 25-person conference room, a computer lab, a student lounge, and an al fresco area to accommodate outdoor events.

Recommendations

Recent years have seen an increase in Native American college student research; this book is just one example. Administrators, staff, and faculty members, including those in NAS, need to educate themselves about the students they serve, all students. A major issue affecting NASSUs is the lack of Native American personnel in the profession and the dearth of professionals who have educated themselves regarding Native American students. Encouraging student affairs or academic affairs staff and faculty to attend conferences and workshops on Native American college students not only will help Native American students, but will also provide professional development for all staff. National organizations like the National Association of Student Personnel Administrators (NASPA) have Native American professionals who can provide resources and contact local Native American communities.

Like all institutional units, NASSUs are subject to assessment. The most appropriate means of assessment would be to create an external review committee made up of other knowledgeable Native American student affairs practitioners to arrange a fair assessment of the program. Some units have set up community advisory councils that can act as sounding boards and assessment boards.

In addition to special advisors, memorandums of understanding (MOUs) developed in collaboration Native communities, TCUs, and the NNI can formalize working agreements. Such MOUs can set goals, encourage communication, and educate both the Native and non-Native community. The University of Idaho, North Idaho College, Lewis-Clark State College, Northwest Indian College, and Washington State University have entered into an MOU to collaborate with a Native American collaborations committee. MOUs and special advisors formalize commitments, identify key individuals, and provide direction.

Conclusion

In this chapter we discussed the difference between NAS and NASSU, the history of NASSUs, and the complicated development that included the varied placement, funding, and administration of these units. We then shared NASSU models as examples and followed this with a short discussion of issues and recommendations. As noted throughout this chapter, NASSUs must work to meet the unique needs of Native students. These students are striving to be human as they journey through an experience that may not always value who they are or what they know. Furthermore, institutions of higher education too often exist without compassion and objectify Native peoples (Davidson, 2008, 2009; McAlpin, 2008). Therefore, spaces are needed for students to experience a sense of cultural safety where the sacred is not suppressed, so they may restore themselves from what can be an exhaustive, insensitive, and treacherous pathway, as a means to reorient themselves to endure the experience of higher education.

Endnotes

1. Please visit www2.ed.gov/about/offices/list/ope/trio/index.html for detailed information.
2. For more information, University of North Dakota American Indian Student Services (2010)
3. Sources for this section include the NASCC website and personal communication with its director, Dean Azule.

References

Astin, A. W. (1993). What matters in college? *Liberal Education, 79*(4), 4–15.
Brown, D. L. (2005). American Indian Student Services at UND. In M. J. T. Fox, S. C. Lowe, & G. S. McClellan (Eds.), *New Directions for Student Services, Serving Native American Students* (Vol. 109, pp. 87–94). San Francisco: Jossey-Bass.

Carney, C. M. (1999). *Native American higher education in the United States.* New Brunswick, NJ: Transaction.

Champagne, D., & Stauss, J. (2002). *Native American Studies in higher education: Models for collaboration between universities and Indigenous nations.* Walnut Creek, CA: AltaMira.

Davidson, C. (2008, September 27). *Truth and tradition: Trusting our histories, stories and ceremonies to decolonize scholarship.* Unpublished paper presented at "In Beauty, It Is Restored: Media Activism, Scholarship & Responsibilities of Indigenous Peoples," Champaign, IL.

Davidson, C. (2009). *Breaking silence: The study of the pervasiveness of oppression.* Unpublished paper presented at the annual meeting of the American Educational Research Association, San Diego, CA.

Emerson, L. W. (2002). HÓZHÓ NÁHÁZDLÍÍ: Towards a practice of Diné decolonization. Unpublished doctoral dissertation, Claremont Graduate University and San Diego State.

Garland, J. L. (2007). [Review of the book *Serving Native American Students: New Directions for Student Services*]. *Journal of College Student Development, 48,* 612–614.

McAlpin, J. D. (2008). *Place and being: Higher education as a site for creating Biskabii—Geographies of indigenous academic identity.* Available from ProQuest Dissertations and Theses database (UMI No. 3314841).

Native American Cultural Center (NACC). (n.d.). *About the program.* Retrieved January 10, 2011, from http://nacc.stanford.edu/program.html

Native American Educational and Cultural Center (NAECC). (2011a). *About NAECC.* Retrieved January 10, 2011, from http://www.purdue.edu/naecc/about.html

Native American Educational and Cultural Center (NAECC). (2011b). *History.* Retrieved January 10, 2011, from http://www.purdue.edu/naecc/history.html

Native American Student and Community Center (NASCC). (2011). Advisory Board bylaws. Retrieved September 1, 2011, from http://www.pdx.edu/nativecenter/advisory-board-0

Native American Student and Community Center (NASCC). (2012). Retrieved from January 2, 2012, http://www.pdx.edu/nativecenter/

Patton, L. D. (2005). Power to the people!: A literature review of the impact of Black student protest on the emergence of Black culture centers. In F. Hord (Ed.), *Black culture centers and political identities* (pp. 151–163). Chicago: Third World.

Patton, L. D., & Hannon, M. D. (2008). Collaboration for cultural programming: Engaging culture centers, multicultural affairs, and student activities offices as partners. In S. R. Harper (Ed.), *Creating inclusive campus environments for cross-cultural learning and student engagement* (pp. 139–154). Washington, DC: NASPA.

Pewewardy, C., & Frey, B. (2004). American Indian students' perceptions of racial climate, multicultural support services, and ethnic fraud at a predominantly White university. *Journal of American Indian Education, 43*(1), 32–60.

Rojas, F. (2007). *From Black power to Black studies: How a radical social movement became an academic discipline.* Baltimore, MD: Johns Hopkins University Press.

Sanford, N. (1962). Developmental status of the entering freshman. In N. Sanford (Ed.), *The American college: A psychological and social interpretation of higher learning* (pp. 253–282). New York: Wiley & Sons.

Shotton, H. S., Yellowfish, S., & Cintrón, R. (2010). Island of sanctuary: The role of an American Indian culture center. In L. Patton (Ed.), *Culture centers in higher education: Perspectives on identity, theory, and practice* (pp. 49–62). Sterling, VA: Stylus.

Smith, L. T. (1999). *Decolonizing methodologies: Research and Indigenous Peoples.* New York: Zed Books.

University of Montana Native American Center. (2012). *Native American Center brochure.* Retrieved November 1, 2012, from http://life.umt.edu/aiss/nac_files/NAC_brochure.pdf

University of North Dakota American Indian Student Services. (2010). Policy on the spiritual use of sage, sweetgrass, and cedar in UND housing, the memorial union, and other nonclassroom buildings. Retrieved from http://www.und.nodak.edu/dept/aiss/sageandsweetgrasspolicy.html

Unser, D. (2001). The American Indian Program at Cornell University. *Indigenous Nations Studies Journal, 2*(1), 35–41.

U.S. Congress. (1998). *Congressional Record. Proceedings and Debates of the 105th Congress, 2nd Session.* 144, Part 16, p. 22687. Washington, DC: Government Printing Office.

Wilkins, D. E. (2002). A tour of Indian peoples and Indian lands. In C. A. Gallagher (Ed.), *Rethinking the color line: Readings in race and ethnicity* (2nd ed.). New York: McGraw-Hill.

Williams, L., & Tanaka, M. (2007). Schalay'nung sxwey'ga: Emerging cross-cultural pedagogy in the academy. *Educational Insights, 11*(3). Retrieved from http://www.ccfi.educ.ubc.ca/publication/insights/vııno3/articles/williams/williams.html

Example Websites for Native American Student Support Unit Models

Cornell University: American Indian Program (AIP) and Akwe:kon
  http://aip.cornell.edu/cals/aip/about/history/index.cfm
Dartmouth University: Native American Program
  http://www.dartmouth.edu/~nap/
Harvard University: Native American Program
  http://www.hunap.harvard.edu/

Portland State University: Native American Student Services and Native American Student Community Center
http://www.pdx.edu/nativecenter/
Purdue University: Native American Educational and Cultural Center
http://www.purdue.edu/naecc/index.html
Stanford University: Native American Cultural Center
http://nacc.stanford.edu/
Syracuse University: Native Student Program
http://multicultural.syr.edu/programs/nsp.html
University of Arizona: Native American Student Affairs
http://nasa.arizona.edu/

8

HOW INSTITUTIONS CAN SUPPORT NATIVE PROFESSIONAL AND GRADUATE STUDENTS

CHiXapkaid (Dr. D. Michael Pavel) (Skokomish)

T his chapter offers perspectives on how institutions of higher education can support Native professional and graduate students. It begins with an overview of the demographic realities described more fully in the introduction chapter to emphasize the importance of institutions establishing a culture of evidence and benchmarks to monitor progress toward increasing student success. The second section provides a personal narrative of lessons learned while working with Native-focused programs. The importance of service learning and professional development opportunities are described in the third section to encourage institutional outreach to Native communities and to facilitate Native graduate student success in advanced degree programs and the transition to the world of work. The final section shares recommendations that are drawn from promising practices in the completion of doctoral programs advocated by the Council of Graduate Schools, research on Native graduate student success, steps to support tribal colleges and universities (TCUs), and embracing a system-wide approach to increasing Native professional and graduate student success.

Demographic Realities

This section provides an overview of Native students in various graduate and professional degree programs. The sources used to glean these findings vary (i.e., they are not always the same), but nevertheless are consistent in portraying the lack of presence of Native students in higher education. For example, Knapp, Kelly-Reid, and Ginder (2010) examined degrees conferred during the 2008–2009 academic year and found that 17,915 Native students received their degrees, mostly from four-year, public institutions (11,804), followed by private, not-for-profit institutions (4,233). A higher percentage of Native women received postbaccalaureate degrees than Native men during the same time period.

The Council of Graduate Schools/GRE Survey of Graduate Enrollment and Degrees also found that Native women (64%) constituted a majority of first-time enrollment in graduate programs (Bell, 2010a). While average annual percentage changes in total enrollment from fall 1999 to fall 2009 were greater for Native women (6.5%) than for Native men (5.2%), Native men experienced a 7.5% increase in first-time enrollment, compared to a 6.1% increase for Native women. Table 8-1 reports that nearly a quarter of American Indian or Alaska Native students in advanced degree programs pursued fields in education, followed by business, natural sciences and engineering, and social and behavioral sciences.

From fall 1999 to fall 2009, the largest average annual percentage change in first-time enrollment was in natural sciences and engineering (8.3%), followed by social sciences and humanities (5.1%), business (5.1%), and education (2.5%). In comparison to changes in total enrollment, the largest increase was in business (7.8%), followed by natural sciences and engineering (6.6%), social sciences and humanities (4.9%), and education (4.4%). Notably, American Indian or Alaska Native student average percentage increases

TABLE 8-1
Percent of First-Time Graduate Enrollment of American Indian or Alaska Native Students by Field of Study, Fall 2009

Field of study	Percent enrollment
Natural sciences & engineering	12%
Social & behavioral sciences	12%
Health sciences	11%
Business	14%
Education	24%
All other fields	28%

Source: Bell, 2010a, p. 11.

for both first-time and total enrollment were higher than for White students, who experienced roughly between 1% and 2% increases (Bell, 2010a). Findings from the National Center for Education Statistics (NCES, 2010a) indicate changes in the number of degrees conferred to American Indian or Alaska Native students between 1997–1998 and 2007–2008. Overall there appears to be a significant increase among Native students receiving bachelor's and master's degrees, but only nominal increases among Native students receiving first-professional and doctoral degrees. More Native women than men received degrees at all levels, except first-professional degrees.

Degrees conferred is the number of students who received a degree, typically within a given academic year. It would be more informative to look at the graduation rates of professional and graduate students. An advanced degree is a minimum requirement for certain occupations (e.g., doctors, lawyers) and is increasingly necessary to attain upper-level positions in many organizations. However, data show that only 40% of American Indians/ Alaska Natives graduated with a bachelor's degree or its equivalent within six years, and American Indians/Alaska Natives consistently had the lowest graduation rates of the five racial/ethnic groups represented in the data (NCES, 2010b). Coupled with the increasing costs of pursing advanced degrees (College Board, 2010), it comes as no surprise that we should be concerned with Native students successfully completing their advanced degree programs in a timely manner.

However, most studies using existing national databases to further understanding of student success have occurred at the undergraduate level. Cook and Pullaro (2010) explain that, "although a significant amount of federal dollars are spent on graduate education, there is currently no federal database that allows for the calculation of a cohort-based graduation rate for graduate education" (p. 22). Bell (2010b) reports Native students are graduating from professional and graduate degree programs at a lower rate than average:

> The median number of years between starting graduate school and receiving the doctoral degree was 7.5. Among US citizen and permanent resident racial/ethnic groups, the median time-to-degree was shortest for multi-race (7.6 years), White (7.7), and Asian (7.7) doctorate recipients, and longest for American Indian [recipients] (9.6). (p. 4)

As such, the logical questions for institutional representatives to ask about professional and graduate programs are, What is the graduation rate for each academic program? What is the Native graduation rate by gender? How does the Native graduation rate compare to the average? What can we do to improve our Native graduation rate? The purpose of asking and answering these types of questions should go beyond reporting statistics to embracing institutional responsibility to measure progress toward advanced degree completion in a timely manner.

As discussed in previous chapters, institutional representatives should also be concerned with increasing the number of Native administrators, faculty, and staff who are involved in the Native culture of an institution of higher education. In fall 2007, less than 1% of college and university faculty were American Indian or Alaska Native (NCES, 2010c). The simple fact is that these low numbers mean Native undergraduates gain little to no exposure to Native role models who understand the path to graduate and professional school. The absence of these role models is not always a deterrent, as some Native students do find other means to fulfill their ambition to successfully pursue an advanced degree. The absence of Native role models is more of a deterrent to institutional commitments to create campuses populated by individuals who have a unique perspective on the challenges, demands, and reality of what it is like to be a Native student (often first-generation) who wants to be a doctor, lawyer, scientist, or professor, or who wants to attain the occupational status defined by being an advanced degree recipient. However, evidence of this sort of institutional commitment can often be found in the stories told about professional and graduate programs specifically tailored to meet the needs of Native students.

Native-Focused Professional and Graduate Programs

The narrative voice is needed to capture the storytelling tradition of Indigenous Peoples. It provides us with an opportunity to share our experiences of working with Native students in institutions of higher education and, from these experiences, glean lessons to guide our future actions. Albeit abbreviated, this story begins at Arizona State University (ASU), moves to the University of California–Los Angeles (UCLA), then to Washington State University (WSU), and now to the University of Oregon (UO). I share my experiences as a graduate student pursuing master's and doctoral degrees, as a tenure-track faculty member, and, finally, as a full professor of Native American studies in education.

As a graduate student at ASU, I, and many other Native graduate students, worked with the Center for Indian Education. *The first lesson I learned is that when faculty members were engaged in our lives we fared much better.* Years later I found this was a delicate dance for Native faculty, who were confronting the full demands of getting tenure and promotion to full professor. *The second lesson learned from this experience was that Native students who showed interest and found time to work directly with faculty played an important role in Native faculty success at a major research university.* Native faculty furthered their relationship with Native students by offering meaningful courses, involving us in projects of interest, personally understanding our ancestral need to be involved with Native communities, and hanging out together at conferences and Native-related events. Overall, my graduate student experience taught me *a third lesson—that shared passion and commitment among highly cooperative colleagues make positive things happen, and Native professional and graduate students benefit greatly from this.*

My first faculty job was at UCLA with a joint appointment in the Higher Education Program and American Indian Studies Center (AISC). The AISC has a well-established reputation for scholarship, teaching, and service. Even so, *the fourth lesson opened my eyes to the reality of politics played out in higher education institutions, and to the fact that politics are an unnecessary struggle we have to endure.* Highly productive and nationally recognized Native faculty still face institutional struggles, and Native professional and graduate students experience the same demands. The AISC met Native student needs by providing resources, opportunities, mentoring, and a safe haven. It is *the fifth lesson learned: that Native-focused programs gave students a place to meet, collaborate with each other and faculty, receive support and encouragement, and enjoy each other's company.*

Several years passed, and I took a faculty position at WSU to move closer to my ancestral home. We started an American Indian Education Initiative in the College of Education, and *the sixth lesson I learned was that institutional support had to involve supporting the Native cultural experience.* For Native students and faculty alike, cultural experiences provided a deep sense of community when people participated in the gatherings. It is at this conscious level that we work together on shared agendas and generate synergy around recruitment, retention, and graduation of Native students at all degree levels.

Now as a full professor of Native American studies in education at UO, I have experienced *the seventh lesson learned in my academic career: to serve the people and the vision of education our ancestors had for us.* Our ancestors wanted us to survive and prosper, but not at the expense of forgetting who we are, where we are from, and our history. We should manifest the vision of our ancestors through the desire of Native-focused program faculty to be engaged in the lives of Native students and that of Native students to actively pursue opportunities to work with faculty. All of us should embrace a sense of passion and commitment, not be discouraged by institutional politics, realize and demand that we have a place at the institution, and support and participate in Native cultural interactions. Of course an institution offering well-established, Native-focused programs would also be characterized by the service-learning and professional development opportunities available to Native professional and graduate students.

Service-Learning and Professional Development

The National Service-Learning Clearinghouse (NSLC, 2009) explains that service learning cultivates civic responsibility when students collaborate with community members to address authentic community needs. Throughout this process, there are opportunities for student development along personal, social, career, and ethical dimensions. This development is facilitated through critical reflection on experiences, curriculum integration, in- and out-of-classroom learning activities, and either individual or group projects. Active learning is optimized, especially when self-engagement and instructional responsibilities are required of the student. Most important is the emphasis on practical problems where Native students play a role in coming up with and carrying out the solutions to challenges confronting Native people.

It is the feeling of doing something worthwhile that is, for Native students, an opportunity to "give back" to their community in an informed, committed, and positive manner (CHiXapkaid & Inglebret, 2007). The act of giving back to their community is one of the central motivations influencing Native students to pursue and obtain postsecondary degrees, motivation that becomes even more essential for students on the journey to complete their advanced degree programs. Success is both an individual and a collective reality. Native students willingly make personal sacrifices on behalf of their families and communities. Additionally, "they see themselves as ready to be role models and decision makers and to implement self-determination. There is an underlying desire to give back to American Indian and Alaska Native peoples and society in general" (pp. 151–152).

Institutions of higher education can feed the spirit of Native professional and graduate students by reaching out to tribes and Native organizations to establish service-learning opportunities. The NSLC offers a number of publications to help institutions of higher education create opportunities for Native students to give back to their communities (www.servicelearning.org /topic/demographics-settings/indian-tribes-us-territories). Service-learning opportunities that cater to community needs and Native national priorities can encourage Native people to decide to pursue a professional or graduate degree and then actually do it. In turn, professional development could help Native students successfully complete advanced degree programs. Professional development is needed in many areas—for example, researching, writing to the audience, time management, technical aspects of particular academic fields, life coaching in the academy, leadership, management, physical/mental well-being, presentations to Native audiences, using technology, networking, grant writing, publishing, preparing curriculum vitae/résumés, interviewing for jobs, and transitioning back to Native communities. Probably one of the most important aspects of any professional development opportunity is to make sure Native students are prepared to use what they have learned to address ongoing issues confronting tribal communities. A host of national organizations is available to provide support:

National Indian Education Association (NIEA)
www.niea.org

American Indian Higher Education Consortium (AIHEC)
www.aihec.org

American Indian Graduate Center (AIGC)
www.aigcs.org

American Indian Science and Engineering Society (AISES)
www.aises.org

National Congress of American Indians (NCAI)
www.ncai.org

Association of American Indian Physicians (AAIP)
www.aaip.org
   Affiliates:

   - Association of Native American Medical Students (ANAMS)
   - Society of American Indian Dentists (SAID)

National Native American Bar Association (NNABA)
www.nativeamericanbar.org

American Indian Council of Architects and Engineers (AICAE)
www.aicae.org

National Association of Student Personnel Administrators (NASPA) and
Indigenous Peoples Knowledge Community (IPKC)
www.naspa.org/kc/ipkc

Recommendations for Practitioners and Institutions

There are many individual and social benefits associated with increasing
Native professional and graduate student success. Baum, Ma, and Payea
(2010) found that individuals with higher levels of education

- earn more and are more likely to be employed;
- are more likely to be satisfied with their jobs;
- are more active citizens, leading to healthier lifestyles; and
- engage in more educational activities with their children.

As Bell (2010c) found, Native students with advanced degrees are sought
after: "American Indian (74%) and white doctorate recipients (72%) were
more likely to have definite [job] commitments than Hispanic (66%), Black
(64%), and Asian (62%) doctorate recipients" (p. 4). The American higher
education community should be resolute in improving Native professional
and graduate student success for the reasons stated previously as well as for
the simple reason that it is the right thing to do. A number of recommendations are advanced to take positive action and to make Native professional
and graduate student success a norm for institutions of higher education in
America.

The first five recommendations are drawn from the Council of Graduate
Schools' (n.d.) PhD completion project undertaken to discern policies and
practices that promote student success. Although the focus is on completing
PhD programs, many of the policies and practices are applicable to professional and master's degree programs: directing attention to important considerations regarding student selection and admissions, mentoring and
advising, financial support, program environment, research experience, and
curricular and administrative processes and procedures. A sixth recommendation is then advanced for practitioners and institutions to view Native
professional and graduate student success in a holistic manner embracing

various dimensions of well-being. Another set of recommendations is presented to address the need for the American higher education community to support TCUs. Finally, a recommendation is advanced for practitioners and institutions to develop viable partnerships within the K–12 arena to ensure that students are prepared for the rigor of pursuing an advanced degree.

Student Selection and Admissions

Institutions wanting to increase Native student admissions and graduation rates will want to ensure that their programs meet the needs of Native students. The institution should have well-established relationships with TCUs and other high-Indian-enrollment institutions. Institutional websites need to include general and Native-related data, information, and resources, and must be clear about what is expected of students to successfully complete the program. The institution should also be in communication with Native applicants and offer professional development opportunities for admissions committees that (a) assess the needs of Native students in relation to the program; (b) determine why admissions offers are accepted or declined by Native applicants; (c) and understand why faculty either support or do not support Native student enrollment.

Mentoring and Advising

Native student success in professional and graduate programs depends on a relationship with one's mentor/advisor that starts early and requires consistent interaction. Enduring and meaningful relationships involve an orientation on what it takes to be successful in the program, a handbook that provides step-by-step direction about what the Native student needs to do, and a checklist of academic milestones that are monitored. This can be complemented by multiple communication channels that Native students and faculty can use to communicate with one another, digital and hard copy portfolios, annual progress reports of academic performance, and mentor/advisor self-assessment of efforts to work with Native students, particularly first-generation Native graduate and professional students.

Financial Support

Financial support is essential to successfully complete a professional or graduate degree program. However, equally important is the need for that financial support to be structured to optimize completion and enhance academic and social integration. Obvious steps include increasing student support in the form of stipends, fellowships, and research awards. Other appealing options are to increase health insurance premiums; establish cost-effective child care; and offer group entertainment events, free supplies and photo-copying, group transportation options, and joint faculty-student awards. Another financial consideration is to offer incentives to departments based on indicators of Native student enrollment and completion.

Program Environment and Research Experience

Professional and graduate program environments that promote Native student success often do so because such advocacy permeates the institutional culture. These institutional cultures are often characterized by campus-wide support networks and services that bring Native students together across disciplines and cultivate community-building activities. Native professional and graduate students are represented on committees at all levels, and institutional efforts are made to engage in public relation campaigns that celebrate Native student achievements and accomplishments. All professional and graduate degree programs involve research, and programs that intend to improve Native student success should provide supportive environments that offer preprogram research experiences and summer institutes. In addition, early research experiences should include opportunities to work with Native communities or on research foci that have relevance to Native people and involve attendance at professional meetings with a Native focus (e.g., NIEA, NCAI, AISES, AIHEC).

Curricular and Administrative Processes and Procedures

Traditional curricular and administrative processes and procedures need to be complemented by new initiatives that support writing and/or preparation for necessary professional certification exams. Web-based systems should be in place to monitor indicators (i.e., beginning with initial contact, application, matriculation, completing of program of study, graduation, and transition to the world of work). Writing assistance for Native professional and graduate students is critical at all stages of an academic program. Support before and during the thesis, dissertation, and required competency exams for professional certification could be facilitated in retreats and institutes that offer uninterrupted time to learn strategies, receive feedback, and cultivate peer support. Consistency can be achieved through a designated room or space that creates an atmosphere where Native students can collaborate with one another.

Have a Holistic View of Success and Persistence Factors

Secatero (2010) found that success and persistence factors for prospective Native professional and graduate students can be explained from a holistic perspective involving eight pillars of well-being:

1. Spiritual Well-being (Purpose): *Why am I attending college?*
2. Cultural Well-being (Identity): *How do I balance my culture and the modern world while I am in college?*
3. Professional Well-being (Planning): *What are the goals for my college and professional career?*
4. Social Well-being (Networking): *Do I have adequate networking skills to succeed in college?*
5. Mental Well-being (Thinking): *Am I academically prepared to meet the rigors of college?*
6. Emotional Well-being (Feeling): *Do I know how to balance my emotions to succeed in college?*
7. Physical Well-being (Body): *Can I take care of myself and my body while I'm in college?*
8. Environmental Well-being (Place): *Is the college that I plan to attend a good fit for me and my goals?*

We can help Native students address each pillar of well-being by answering the relevant questions and reflecting critically on their knowledge of available resources, awareness of personal strengths/attributes, ability to identify challenges, and propensity to develop a plan of action. The Native students should take personal responsibility to know what is a resource, how to access resources, and then take advantage of any resource that will help them succeed. This is supported by their ability to recognize and honor personal strengths and positive attributes, and acknowledge these strengths/attributes every day. Each individual Native student needs to identify any and all challenges that might become obstacles in order to succeed in his or her advanced degree program. The ultimate step, then, is to develop a plan of action that helps the Native student successfully navigate the journey to completing an advanced degree program.

Support Tribal Colleges and Universities

TCUs have been successful at improving the educational attainment and employment prospects of American Indians and Alaska Natives by offering higher education that is culturally relevant and connected to the needs of tribal communities. The collective American higher education community and various levels of government should support efforts to increase TCU capacity to meet the needs of Native professional and graduate students. To build on the success of TCUs and TCU graduates, practitioners and institutions can support efforts to

- Increase philanthropic giving to TCUs, increase student scholarships, and improve and expand TCU offerings and facilities;
- Increase federal and state governments' investment in TCUs to help more American Indian students attend college and earn a degree;
- Enhance the capacity of TCUs to offer more distance-learning opportunities, enhance student services, expand service-learning opportunities, and establish networks with TCU alumni;
- Continue outreach to alumni and scholarship recipients, monitor their progress, celebrate their achievements, and encourage their participation in follow-up activities; and
- Conduct collaborative research on the transition from TCUs to other types of institutions.

A final recommendation for practitioners and institutions is to develop viable partnerships within the K–12 arena to ensure that students are prepared for the rigors of pursuing an advanced degree. For example, American Indians or Alaska Natives accounted for 16,000, or 1.3%, of the 1,206,000 high school graduates who took the ACT. Of these Native students, approximately 60% "took at least a minimum core high school curriculum to prepare them for college (defined as four years of English and three years each of mathematics, social studies, and science)" (ACT, 2010, p. 4). Expanding our vision to improve K–12 offerings allows us to focus on the opportunity to seek system-wide changes that result in greater gains. Conley (2010) agrees that we should be teaching students knowledge and skills for college and career readiness, and then he offers evidence for why high schools need to change their focus through practical methods to enhance the readiness of their students. There is something appealing about being able to focus on a high leverage point, such as improving education institutions, rather than simply adhering to a deficit strategy of improving the individual Native student.

Conclusion

How can institutions support Native professional and graduate students? If institutional representatives are serious and sincere enough to ask such a question, then the answer should begin with, "We can and should support Native professional and graduate students." The world of higher education is replete with smart people who know the value of being forward thinking when looking at the low number of Native people who aspire to complete advanced degree programs. Such people know and appreciate the value of stories that attest to the benefit of Native graduate and professional programs. Personnel at all institutional levels should demonstrate the willingness to be aware of Native issues and carry out the initiative to become involved in Native-related organizations that address these issues. It becomes evident to everyone who cares that investment and efforts need to be made to embrace service-learning and professional development opportunities. Supporting Native graduate and professional students simply means focusing on reasonable, manageable, and doable recommendations that are drawn from promising practices. We are that smart, we can be that dedicated, and we can ask such a question courageously and answer it with action.

References

ACT. (2010). *The condition of college & career readiness 2010.* Iowa City, IA: Author.

Baum, S., Ma, J., & Payea, K. (2010). *Education pays 2010: The benefits of higher education for individuals and society.* New York: The College Board Advocacy & Policy Center.

Bell, N. (2010a). *Graduate enrollment and degrees: 1999 to 2009.* Washington, DC: Council of Graduate Schools.

Bell, N. (2010b, March). Data sources: Time-to-degree for doctorate recipients. *Communicator, 43*(2), pp. 4–5.

Bell, N. (2010c, July). Employment trends among new doctorate recipients. *Communicator, 43*(6), p. 4–5.

CHiXapkaid (Pavel, D. M.) & Inglebret, E. (2007). *The American Indian and Alaska Native student's guide to college success.* Westport, CT: Greenwood.

College Board. (2010). Trends in college pricing 2010. New York: College Board Advocacy & Policy Center.

Conley, D. (2010). *College and career ready.* San Francisco: Jossey-Bass.

Cook, B., & Pullaro, N. (2010, September). *Graduation rates: Behind the numbers.* Washington, DC: American Council on Education.

Council of Graduate Schools. (n.d.). *Ph.D. completion project: Policies and practices to promote student success,* Executive Summary. Retrieved December 26, 2010, from http://www.phdcompletion.org/information/Executive_Summary_Student_Success_Book_IV.pdf

Knapp, L. G., Kelly-Reid, J. E., & Ginder, S. A. (2010). *Postsecondary institutions and price of attendance in the United States: Fall 2009, degrees and other awards conferred: 2008–09, and 12-Month Enrollment: 2008–09* (NCES 2010-161, p. 11). Washington, DC: National Center for Education Statistics, U.S. Department of Education. Retrieved December 21, 2010, from http://nces.ed.gov/pubsearch/pubsinfo.asp?pubid = 2010161

National Center for Education Statistics (NCES). (2010a). *Condition of education 2010* (NCES 2010-028). Washington, DC: U.S. Department of Education, Table A-23-2.

National Center for Education Statistics (NCES). (2010b). *Digest of education statistics, 2009* (NCES 2010-013). Washington, DC: U.S. Department of Education, Table 246. Retrieved December 23, 2010, from http://nces.ed.gov/fastfacts/display.asp?id = 61

National Center for Education Statistics (NCES). (2010c). *The condition of education 2010* (NCES 2010-028), Indicator 21. Retrieved December 21, 2010, from http://nces.ed.gov/fastfacts/display.asp?id = 40

National Service-Learning Clearinghouse (NSLC). (2009). Retrieved from http://www.servicelearning.org/instant_info/fact_sheets/tribal_facts/americorps_and_service-learning_101

Secatero, S. L. (2010). *American Indian well-being model in higher education.* Paper prepared for the 4th International Indigenous Conference, Matauranga Taketake: Traditional Knowledge 2010 Conference, Auckland, New Zealand.

9

FANCY WAR DANCING ON ACADEME'S GLASS CEILING

Supporting and Increasing Indigenous Faculty
Role Models in Higher Education

Dr. Cornel Pewewardy (Comanche/Kiowa)

In the title of this chapter, the term "fancy war dancing" is a pow-wow metaphor to convey what many Indigenous students and faculty feel they need to do to earn a college degree or earn promotion and tenure at mainstream universities; they have to perform a fancy war dance, skip dance, or jump through hoops at warp-speed pace, conscious that missing a beat will result in failure. Given that Indigenous students have the highest dropout rates compared to other ethnic groups in higher education, one strategy for recruiting and retaining Indigenous students in colleges and universities is to recruit, retain, and promote more Indigenous faculty members simply because they instantly serve as role models to Indigenous students. This strategy also promotes such principles as sustainability and diversity in a university's overall strategic goals. Mainstream educators must always be mindful of and become familiar with the importance of recruiting Indigenous role models in higher education institutions, especially at non-Native colleges and universities (NNCUs).

When I went up for promotion and tenure to full professor, I could think of only five Indigenous full professors nationwide who could be eligible to serve as external reviewers for my promotion and tenure materials. Of those five, only one had a similar portfolio to mine: Indigenous education and culture. To me, there is a difference between Indigenous urban education and reservation or rural-based education. Far too often, faculty doing research in the field of Indigenous education have focused on reservation or rural-based education. Having worked and lived in both urban and reservation-based environments, I recognize that there are significant living and working experiences that affect teaching and learning, such as road conditions, transportation, dialectical communications, access to libraries and technology, knowledge and use of tribal ceremonies, access to health care, resident tribal members versus absentee tribal members, to name just a few.

Many Indigenous students say they have "to find their own way" through college, especially those attending NNCUs. Because most Indigenous students are first-generation college students, they have few role models in their tribal communities to help them navigate the maze of college life and culture. While greater numbers of Indigenous students have enrolled in colleges and universities over the years, first-generation college student status has contributed to decades of difficult adjustment from supportive tribal communities to new sociocultural higher education environments. At the same time, most colleges and universities have lacked the institutional support networks to recruit, retain, and support Indigenous students. As a result, Indigenous faculty in higher education are scarce (Turner & Myers, 2000), thereby reducing the academic pool of faculty available to mentor Indigenous students.

This chapter discusses the complicated issue of Indigenous role models in higher education. For this chapter, role models are described as Indigenous, tenure-track, or tenured faculty members at NNCUs. An Indigenous role model on an NNCU campus can be defined in ways that further colonization, such as ignoring Indigenous Knowledge Systems in favor of mainstream dominant ones. I share my experiences in an effort to serve as a positive role model for Indigenous students and tenure-seeking faculty members who often confront racist and unfriendly campus environments.

Shortage of Indigenous Faculty to Serve as Role Models

Increasing the numbers of faculty of color is an ongoing challenge for higher education institutions (Stanley, 2006). According to Trower and Chait (2002), African American, Hispanic, and Native American faculty constituted only 5% of the full professors in the United States. The number of Native American faculty has always been low (Garcia, 2000; Snyder & Hoffman, 2001; Turner, 2002). Pavel, Swisher, and Ward (1994) found that the proportion of American Indian and Alaska Native full-time faculty increased slightly, from 0.3% to 0.4% between 1981 and 1991, and the *Chronicle of Higher Education*'s *Almanac of Higher Education* (2011) reported that American Indian full-time faculty at the professor level account for no more than 0.5% of the total faculty population. The slight increases in faculty were seen in NNCUs, but also in tribal colleges (Warner & Gipp, 2009). Cross and Shortman's (1995) demographic analysis of tribal college faculty underscores the need to increase the number of American Indian and Alaska Native faculty. These data show that faculty of color, particularly Indigenous faculty, are not reflective of U.S. society as a whole.

Indigenous students must see (witness) and interact with Indigenous faculty on campus to introduce them to the possibility of becoming future faculty members. Indigenous faculty members can provide much-needed mentoring and often motivate Indigenous students to attain their college or university goals. Having visible Indigenous role models is critical for Indigenous students, and the earlier these are introduced to Indigenous faculty, the better. Let me give you an example of what I try to do when I talk with young Indigenous students about the people who influence their lives. If I ask Indigenous students to name five famous adult athletes or five famous movie stars, they most likely will name them with no problem at all. However, when I ask those same Indigenous students to name five Indigenous faculty members or Indigenous men with college degrees, they mostly likely will be challenged to answer that question. To me, this illustrates the importance of identifying Indigenous role models in higher education today, because having Indigenous role models could strongly influence the self-concept and self-esteem of young Indigenous students. Over the years, I have found the most important factor affecting the academic achievement of today's Indigenous students is teacher expectations and support.

The person who stands out as my key lifetime Indigenous faculty role model was Dr. Mike Charleston.[1] Mike was a member of the Choctaw Nation and was director of and associate professor in the American Indian Leadership Program at Pennsylvania State University. His thirst for quantitative research was admirable and one that I have not seen matched since. What moved me was his ability to speak his Choctaw language fluently, an amazing cultural trait rarely demonstrated among Indigenous faculty members today. He also was a traditional Straight Dancer of the Southern Plains traditions in Oklahoma. Mike recruited me to the doctoral program in educational administration at Pennsylvania State University, because he believed in my potential and desire to succeed in a doctoral program of advanced study. Most important, he taught me that it makes no sense for an Indigenous academic to begin an intellectual quest from someone else's standpoint, that is, from another ethnic group's perspective.

Developing Critical Consciousness

My critical consciousness was awakened during my doctoral studies while I was taking classes in educational foundations and policy. Professors at the Pennsylvania State University introduced me to the primary works of Brazilian thinker Paulo Freire. This was my first concentrated introduction to critical race theory and pedagogy. Since then, my work has been inspired by Indigenous scholars like Vine Deloria Jr., Elizabeth Cook-Lynn, Linda Tuhiwai Smith, Jeff Corntassel, Waziyatawin Angela Wilson, Michael Yellow Bird, Robert Porter, Devon Mihesuah, and Taiaiake Alfred. Within this group of courageous scholars, I found a circle of Indigenous mentors and colleagues who understood how Indigenous Peoples were miseducated about their tribal cultures and how learning could be liberating. Already deeply politicized before graduate school, I had no difficulty embracing a Freirean approach to my teaching, research, and service in higher education.

 During my early years in higher education, I found only a few Indigenous faculty members writing about social justice issues. Most Indigenous scholars were writing about non–social justice issues such as Indian health, the status of Indian education, or tribal identity construction. Centering more on a "how can we all get along" multicultural discourse, these disciplines did not challenge the status quo or liberate critical thinking. I was not discouraged, however, and my lifetime commitment to social justice continues today, because it was inspired by former professors and teachers who helped me develop my own pedagogical practice of freedom.

The Role Model Argument—"I'm Not Your Indian Anymore"

Years ago I wrote a poem, titled "BIA (Bureau of Indian Affairs), I'm Not Your Indian Anymore," that was inspired by hearing a "49" song composed and sung by the late Floyd "Red Crow" Westerman, a Lakota political activist and actor.[2] Following are some insights into why I do not see myself as a role model as framed from a mainstream perspective:

 Insight 1: Being an Indigenous role model on a mainstream college campus is a very difficult task that requires long hours of study, research, and overcommitment, which can cause serious health problems. Some Indigenous role model perceptions are that you are expected to liberate your tribal people from all of their social and psychological ills, often placing their needs before your own.

Insight 2: Mainstream colleagues encourage and may want to take advantage of your diverse status by expecting you to serve as faculty advisor and mentor to all the Indigenous students, give talks all over campus, serve on scores of diversity committees and panels, and be available to serve the university in countless ways other faculty do not.

Insight 3: Indigenous faculty role model concepts are unclear, and you are often expected to advocate for all the underrepresented and underserved populations on campus.

Insight 4: Indigenous role models are expected to assimilate into mainstream academic culture. This can mean not challenging the bureaucracy and structures of the university; not being a radical activist; not bringing to campus any traditional medicines, like sweetgrass, smudge sticks, tobacco, rattles, or drums; and not chanting/praying in your office, in the classroom, or in meetings. Indigenous men would also not wear their hair long or colorfully braided, would not wear any type of earrings, and would not have tattoos or body piercings.

Insight 5: Being a good role model in academe means having to stand up to society's very high moral expectations. This is very difficult for many Indigenous faculty today, especially me. As human beings, many of us have made human mistakes in our lives, mostly when we were young. Consequently, a phenomenon that many Indigenous professionals have to deal with is the Indian crab theory.[3] Another conundrum is to tell younger Indigenous people that if they work hard in their studies, stay out of trouble from the law, practice their traditional ways, and speak their tribal languages, they can be a professor like me. Why would I want any graduate student to go through a grinding academic process like I did, confronting increased racial hostility, cultural slurs, and ethnic harassment?

Dealing With Racism and Uncollegial Behavior

It might be hard for a graduate student or new faculty member to understand why anyone would not support an academic career in higher education. This is especially significant given the emphasis on diversifying faculty and affirming diversity on college campuses. Despite the rhetoric on diversity, however, many professors, administrators, and publishers can still act as gatekeepers in higher education. Even stories of intertribal racism exist within higher education.

I tell students that, even if they find an Indigenous faculty member in higher education, it does not mean the faculty member will advocate for Indigenous students or for them in college. Over the course of my career in higher education, I have discovered that we (Indigenous faculty) cannot be the cure (decolonization) if we are the disease (colonization). According to Wilson and Yellow Bird (2005),

> decolonization is the intelligent, calculated, and active resistance to the forces of colonialism that perpetuate the subjugation and/or exploitation of our minds, bodies, and lands, and it is engaged for the ultimate purpose of overturning the colonial structure and realizing Indigenous liberation. (p. 2)

Therefore, I see the antidote to colonization for Indigenous Peoples as decolonization. It involves working with our allies and our students as well as within the circles of Indigenous faculty in higher education. It is certainly a lifelong career challenge, one we cannot take on alone and unsupported by the institutions where we do our work in academe.

Uncollegial behavior by colleagues of all colors comes in many shapes and forms and at various department levels. I can think of three broad categories of uncollegial behavior: verbal attacks, destructive game playing, and withholding support. Verbal attacks consist of oral or written communication that belittles, humiliates, or shames the recipient of the communication. Destructive game playing is an ongoing series of complementary ulterior transactions progressing to a well-defined, predictable outcome. For example, when I was hired in a tenure-track faculty position at a predominantly White Carnegie research I university in the Midwest, I found myself in the elevator with the university's chief legal counsel. Without any greeting or introduction in the elevator, he leaned over to me and said, "Just keep us [the university] out of the courts." He then walked quickly out of the elevator as if nothing had happened and hurried on his way across campus. This gesture proved his lack of support and could be defined as failure to assist or protect colleagues when they are being treated unfairly or withholding words or actions that encourage or compliment the hard work, efforts, accomplishments, or courageous risks taken by colleagues.

Last year at Portland State University, I was awarded full professor status, thereby achieving academic success from a mainstream university perspective. However, this lifelong task came with mixed feelings because of the many inequalities I had to overcome in my tenure-track journey in academe. Like Caroline Turner and Samuel Myers (2000), I found achieving tenure to be a bittersweet success in academe, because it took decades to get four university degrees and travel the ranks of academe, all while confronting my own personal trials and tribulations along the way. For most of my career in higher education, I have had to battle against a current of subtle discrimination. Although I want to encourage Indigenous students and junior faculty to join the professoriate, there are many personal stories of struggle by Indigenous faculty that prohibit and intimidate pursuing a career in mainstream academe.

Ethnic Fraud in Higher Education

The current economic upheaval has contributed to an increase in social turbulence faced by both graduate students and new faculty members in higher education. Consequently, new faculty members can expect to encounter increased tension and, often, hostile working environments because of fierce competition for scarce resources. The change in the makeup of new faculty of color and the tenuous economic conditions have caused a growing uneasiness on the part of those who are employed. Changing the ethnic face of higher education has also brought a need for working relationships grounded in effective and supportive cultural interactions. Unfortunately, it seems that diversifying the color of the faculty has instead increased the likelihood of racial tension, gatekeeping strategies, and increased institutional racism.

Cultural exploitation has found its way into faculty applications and searches in higher education. Prominent examples of ethnic fraud are individual candidates who self-identify as American Indian or Alaska Native by checking the appropriate race box while consciously knowing they cannot provide evidence to meet many tribal enrollment requirements. An example of cultural exploitation that affects all students is falsification of ethnic identity to be eligible for scholarships, staff and faculty employment applications, and promotions. Many students and faculty who are able to present documented cases for employment, promotion, or scholarships are passed over because institutions do not have a process in place to screen the authenticity of tribal identity. Individuals may engage in ethnic fraud because they know most higher education officials will never verify their tribal membership. Even though many non-Indigenous applicants have been exposed, unless universities are willing to create and follow established guidelines, and unless tribes complain more aggressively when they discover someone pretending to be of their tribal group, fraudulent behavior will continue and even proliferate in higher education.

The Evolution of Diasporic Identities: Contrasting Tribal Reservation and "Urban Rez" Consciousness

Having experienced a lifetime of working and living in both tribal college communities and urban university environments, I believe our response to the state of Indigenous education ultimately must target ideology and structures, not merely everyday individual behavior. Indigenous academics should know the history, purposes, consequences, and structures of the racial paradigm. I believe individuals who see themselves as cultural beings are not intimidated by others who claim cultural supremacy and hegemony. Moreover, I believe Indigenous academics should be engaged in consciously dismantling a settler paradigm. Finally, I believe we should help to heal the soul wound of Indigenous Peoples (Duran, 2006).

Indigenous Peoples have always faced and solved their educational problems and socialization as a greater part of an evolving Indigenous cultural consciousness. As I synthesize my discussion of Indigenous history and culture, my conscious attempt is not to approach it merely as an individual of Indigenous descent, but rather from an evolving tribal consciousness that synthesizes the history and culture, ancient and modern, of Indigenous Peoples within the Western diaspora, specifically the United States. It is within this context that I am interested in Indigenizing educational designs and socialization processes of Indigenous Peoples. How did Indigenous Peoples educate themselves in traditional ways? What were the purposes, methodologies, pedagogy, epistemologies, and content of Indigenous learning systems?

Not all Indigenous People were raised or live on reservation-based communities. Most Indigenous Peoples today live in urban communities. Accordingly, I find that many students, and especially Indigenous faculty in urban universities, have frail connections with their genealogical tribal communities. Of course, much of their tribal identity disconnection is the result of the U.S. government's attempt to urbanize Indigenous Peoples and encourage cultural assimilation mainly into large urban communities. To resist assimilation into urban communities, many Indigenous Peoples created Indigenous enclaves and diasporic identities. Therefore, urban Indigenous identity may be in a transitional stage in the evolution of tribal identity.

Cultural Being in Higher Education

If new faculty downplay socialization and service, they increase their risk of getting a poor start in their academic careers. What most tenured faculty look for in new faculty is the ability to work and socialize with them for many years. Given the customary ambiguity about socialization and service, few new Indigenous faculty can model good collegial behavior while retaining their individuality. Brown, Guy, and McClennan (1999) contend that, as faculty of color, we cannot conceal our individual identities in higher education, but rather speak of ourselves and encourage our students to do the same. Personally, I have a life outside of the ivory tower as I continually practice learning the traditional songs of my tribes and singing annually at our traditional pow-wows in Oklahoma and the Southwest. Even though I live thousands of miles away from my tribal homeland, I return constantly to return the gift of my education through my learning songs and dances.

Role Molding

Perhaps the next step for Indigenous faculty is to move beyond role modeling to role molding. Brown et al. (1999) contends that one serves as a symbolic figure of what is possible or aspired to; however, "role molding is the active engagement of faculty in shaping the lives of their students into the academic and social shapes or pattern which the students desire" (p. 115). For example, early in my academic career I noticed that most Indigenous male faculty members did not keep their hair long, wear earrings, practice their traditional tribal ceremonies, speak their tribal languages, or stay in touch with tribal communities. Another case in point came from a current student of mine who asked me for a letter of recommendation, which I agreed to. I was surprised to find that he had cut his long, dark hair. He told me, "I cut my hair to get a job." I was taken aback by his actions. For all purposes of this discussion about cultural beings, some individuals have chosen to assimilate into mainstream's "good old White boy" network to succeed in their academic careers. This has never been my practice. I know my career's academic agenda has not been a popular one, especially in educational policy, because of my stand on tribal sovereignty and self-determination. To me, being true to your cultural being is the practice of freedom.

Creating Holistic Energy

For Indigenous faculty members to succeed in higher education, they have to be holistic. This means having constant high energy and the ability to mix Western education and medicine with traditional Indigenous healing methods. Positive energy comes from honoring the Earth and its creatures, developing a capacity for tolerance, and having the passion to achieve a peaceful civilization. Being successful means learning to balance your energy.

Being born and raised in my tribal community afforded me an opportunity to learn culture and tribal languages from my family, extended family, and close tribal friends. Having political influence in the tribe has helped tremendously as well. Being called upon for ceremony and song, as well as consultation of tribal traditions, helps ground my identity within my tribal homelands. Observing many students, staff, and faculty in urban communities explore their personal quest for a tribal identity in higher education, I see a pattern of forging diasporic identities, one that tries to merge an absentee tribal identity (removed from traditional homelands) with an evolving urban Indigenous consciousness. Identity issues are enormous for Indigenous Peoples in higher education. No ethnic group has endured a longer external assault on its spirit like that of Indigenous Peoples. These are tribal family issues that need to be resolved within the tribal families. On the other hand, equity requires our collective and immediate attention.

Abundant oral and written records exist to describe the educational history of Indigenous Peoples, especially its ancient and traditional forms. These ancient traditions are profound models of culturally responsive excellence in Indigenous education. The basic path of my career in higher education has always been to live what I teach. I have not had an easy life overall, especially in higher education. I have failed at many things, but I have learned many lessons from failure. My own healing path has required reconciling intuitions, such as empathy, with medical science and Western educational theories. Developing positive energy is about knowing your natural rhythms and becoming familiar with your working environment.

Balancing academic work with a personal life has always been a challenge for me as an Indigenous academic. As faculty, we try to create an environment where our students will aspire to serve comparable roles in the lives of future students. Because Indigenous students almost always need financial assistance, Indigenous faculty often become the "anonymous donor" for books, food, and other educational needs. Therefore, to share a faculty member's career and personal self at this academic level requires academics to be balanced holistically to allow faculty to maintain their integrity.

Conclusion

I wrote this chapter for all of those graduate students who felt the odds were against them in their pursuit of an academic career in higher education.

Moreover, I wrote this chapter for those Indigenous colleagues in academe who struggle every day to win acceptance and success in their faculty positions, but still wonder how they have succeeded without having to give up their cultural identities and tribal languages—that is, fundamentally assimilating their tribal identity toward mainstream academe. And I wrote this chapter for those Indigenous colleagues who have already sacrificed layers of their cultural identity in their quest for promotion and tenure and wonder now how they can ever recover the tribal cultures and languages they have lost along the way. Many of these academic "survivors" ask the question: What does it take for Indigenous faculty to achieve and prosper in the academy?

It is up to all Indigenous faculty to do our part to continue to make progress. The current and next generation of Indigenous scholars will have more advantages in this regard than those faculty members whose accomplishments we celebrate today. They will likely have spouses and partners who are more committed to the dual-career model than was evident in the past, and societal norms will support their professional pursuits more fully. They will have a clear awareness of the barriers that continue to exist and will work at institutions whose leadership is fully committed to achieving parity and equitable representation for Indigenous faculty.

Endnotes

1. Dr. G. Mike Charleston passed away in his mid-40s from cancer.
2. "49" songs are social songs usually sung after pow-wows or at a location where people can have a good time singing and dancing after the sun goes down.
3. Like the metaphor of crabs in a bucket: once a crab has climbed to the top and is ready to climb out, there is another crab or two waiting to grab hold and pull the ascending crab down to the bottom of the bucket.

References

Brown, M. C., Guy, L. D., & McClennan, S. A. (1999). Mentoring graduate students of color: Myths, models, and modes. *Peabody Journal of Education, 74*(2), 105–118.

Chronicle of Higher Education. (2011). *Almanac of Higher Education.* Retrieved from http://chronicle.com/section/Almanac-of-Higher-Education/615/

Cross, K. P., & Shortman, P. V. (1995, Summer). Tribal college faculty: The demographics. *Tribal College,* 34–37.

Duran, E. (2006). *Healing the soul wound: Counseling with American Indians and other native peoples.* New York: Teachers College Press.

Garcia, M. (2000). *Succeeding in an academic career: A guide for faculty of color.* Westport, CT: Greenwood.

Pavel, D. M., Swisher, K., & Ward, M. (1994). Special focus: American Indian and Alaska native demographic and educational trends. *Minorities in Higher Education, 13,* 33–56.

Snyder, T. D., & Hoffman, C. M. (2001). *Digest of education statistics, 2000* (NCES 2001-034). Washington, DC: U.S. Department of Education, National Center for Education Statistics.

Stanley, C. A. (2006). *Faculty of color: Teaching in predominantly white colleges and universities.* Bolton: Anker Publishing.

Trower, C. A., & Chait, R. P. (2002). Faculty diversity: Too little for too long. *Harvard Magazine, 104*(4), 33–37, 98.

Turner, C. S. V. (2002). *Diversifying the faculty: A guidebook for search committees.* Washington, DC: Association of American Colleges and Universities Publications.

Turner, C. S. V., & Myers, S. L. (2000). *Faculty of color in academe: Bittersweet success.* Boston: Allyn & Bacon.

Warner, L. S., & Gipp, G. E. (2009). *Tradition and culture in the millennium: Tribal colleges and universities.* Charlotte, NC: Information Age.

Wilson, W. A., & Yellow Bird, M. (2005). *For Indigenous eyes only: A decolonization handbook.* Santa Fe, NM: School of American Research.

10

BEST PRACTICES FOR NATIONAL ORGANIZATIONS TO SUPPORT THE NATIVE EXPERIENCE IN HIGHER EDUCATION

Dr. John L. Garland (Choctaw) and Dr. George S. McClellan

P rofessional associations in student affairs can and should play an important role in supporting student affairs professionals in efforts to address racial and ethnic differences in higher education. This chapter explores the role of professional associations in assisting student affairs professionals to fulfill their role supporting the success of Native American students, staff, and faculty in higher education. This exploration begins with a review of the historical roots of professional associations in student affairs and then addresses the interaction between social movements and professional associations. Next, the chapter includes a discussion of the contemporary roles of professional associations, particularly those in student affairs. The chapter then presents an overview of the involvement of Native Americans in various associations and provides practical examples for future consideration.

Today there are over 20 national associations associated with student affairs and its functional areas. The groups and their histories mentioned in this chapter are not meant to be an exhaustive listing, but are rather meant to provide context when considering Native American participation in higher education's student affairs professional organizations.

Roots of the Professional Associations

Initially formed as associations for deans of women and men, student affairs professional associations now represent national, regional, and functional interests. Two of the dominant professional associations affiliated with student affairs professionals include American College Personnel Association (ACPA)–College Student Educators International, and National Association of Student Personnel Administrators (NASPA)–Student Affairs Administrators in Higher Education. While these two organizations are the largest professional associations representing student affairs practice nationally, functional areas of student affairs practice, interest areas, and associations representing historically underrepresented groups in higher education also maintain highly respected and nationally prominent organizations, as is discussed later in this chapter.

Since the founding of the first professional society in 1743 by Benjamin Franklin, professional organizations and associations in the United States have come to resemble the institutional and individual members associated with them. Nuss (1996) notes,

> Racial barriers and discrimination prevented the full participation of minorities in these [student affairs] professional associations. . . . Over time, the other [nonethnically based] student affairs professional associations became more accepting of minorities. Not until 1976, however, did an African American, Anne Pruitt, become president of ACPA, and not until 1985 was an African American, Bob Leach, elected to serve as NASPA president. (pp. 30–31)

According to Moore and Neuberger (1998, p. 72), "diversity in membership and programs has been expressed as a priority" by the major professional associations in student affairs.

Membership demographics in both ACPA and NASPA represent, in part, the feminization of the student affairs profession (McEwen, Williams, & Engstrom, 1991). Data reported in 2011 show that the majority of members (60%) in both associations are female. Membership of both associations is also predominantly White. African Americans and Hispanic Americans are the second- and third-most represented ethnic groups in each association, and Native Americans are the least-represented ethnic group in both associations. Native Americans make up just over 0.5% of the combined membership of ACPA and NASPA, with the two associations reporting 24 and 76 Native American members, respectively. Some caution must be taken, however, with respect to the information regarding ethnic participation in ACPA and NASPA, given that both associations have significant percentages of nonresponses regarding ethnicity in their membership data (data reported by NASPA and ACPA in 2011).

Social Movements and the Associations

The nature and development of professional associations and their functions also reflect the context of U.S. history. Institutions of higher education (IHEs) and their professional associations, including those representing student affairs fields, are often engaged in the broader societal struggles of their time. National movements such as those affiliated with equal rights for women, civil rights for African Americans, American Indian sovereignty, and so on, are often represented within professional organizations by those associated with the movements.

These and other movements for equality and recognition, prompted by histories of separation, marginalization, and oppression of particular citizens within our society, resulted in distinct interest groups emerging and evolving over time. Organizations representing these groups were frequently developed as freestanding associations or as subgroups within the larger majority representative organizations. For example, the National Association of Student Affairs Professionals (NASAP), a historically African American organization, traces its roots to the Advisors of Girls in Colored Schools and the Deans of Men in Negro Education Institutions (Nuss, 2000, p. 494).

Roles of Professional Associations

In reflecting on the ways in which professional associations in student affairs may help in efforts to facilitate the success of Native American students, staff, and faculty, it is important to consider first the roles of these organizations. According to Nuss (2003), professional associations

> seek to advance understanding, recognition, and knowledge in the field; to develop and promulgate standards for professional practice; to inform the public on key issues; to stimulate and organize volunteers; and to provide professionals with a peer group that promotes a sense of identity. (p. 493)

Hunter and Comey (1991) write, "The evolution of a professional identity for student affairs workers (literally what it means to be 'one of us') is linked to socialization into the professional culture and mastery of its knowledge base" (p. 11). Schrank and Young (1987) assert, "Professional associations can individually (or, more ideally, collectively) affect the success of professional education [on] individual campuses, in states, in regions, [and] at the national level" (p. 64).

Moore and Neuberger (1998) note, however, that "[a]ssociations have provided important continuing professional education both to the membership and to higher education in general. Depending on the issue, however, the quality, timeliness and relevance of their response has varied" (p. 71). In addition to the role associations play in shaping and providing professional education, Moore and Neuberger (1998) report,

> Professional associations strive to remain current with [societal influences and institutional issues facing student affairs practitioners] and develop responses in a timely fashion. . . . The more critical the issue is to the survival of the institutional or individual member, the more important the role of the professional association becomes in responding to the member. (p. 65)

According to Hunter and Beeler (1991), "Professional associations affiliated with student affairs are in the powerful position to link student affairs workers who vary in terms of seniority, functional areas, institutional settings, or geography" (pp. 117–118).

Finally, student affairs professional associations have identified diversity as a societal influence and institutional issue facing student affairs practitioners, and have developed lists of expected competencies for new student affairs professionals that include competencies as facilitators of multicultural environments and as change agents (Evans & Williams, 1998). Pope, Reynolds, and Cheatham (1997) report that "woven into the core values of the ACPA–College Student Educators International, is a strong commitment to multiculturalism, inclusiveness, and human dignity" (p. 62). They argue that ACPA can fill the void in knowledge and practice regarding diversity and pluralism. In addition, NASPA's (1987) *A Perspective on Student Affairs*, one of the association's core documents, addresses the importance of understanding each student as unique and of actively opposing bigotry.

In sum, the list of identified roles for student affairs professional associations includes the following:

- Promote understanding and recognition in the field,
- Encourage the development and dissemination of knowledge related to the field,

- Define professional competencies for the field,
- Shape professional preparation programs for the field,
- Facilitate socialization of new members into the field,
- Advance professional development of members of the field,
- Foster a sense of unity and identity for the field, and
- Articulate and advocate for social dimensions of practice in the field.

While these roles are somewhat generic, the following sections contain information that may identify areas in which these roles have practical applications.

Native Americans and the Indigenization of Student Affairs

NASPA and ACPA each includes within its organization groups that share common interests and affiliation within student affairs. Specifically related to Native American- and ally-focused groups, NASPA has the Indigenous Peoples Knowledge Community (IPKC), and ACPA has the Native American Network (NAN). Both groups also work together in collaboration through what is known as the NANIPKC (pronounced nan-i-pik) to outline broad initiatives and to sustain community within higher education. Each group has its own mission and organizational structure. IPKC's stated mission is as follows:

> The Indigenous Peoples Knowledge Community (IPKC) is an all-inclusive group of student affairs professionals and students identifying as Native American/First Nations/Alaskan Native/Native Hawaiian heritage, including international indigenous nations, and any persons with a shared concern about the betterment of indigenous students in higher education. . . .
>
> The IPKC actively promotes the empowerment of NASPA members through education, research, shared knowledge, mentoring initiatives, and online forums about Indigenous issues. The IPKC's goals are to inform about current issues, trends, nurturing and promoting the advancement of Indigenous professionals and encourage Indigenous college students to consider student affairs as a profession.
>
> A primary mission is to increase the IPKC members' awareness of, knowledge about, shared concern for, and appreciation for issues unique to Indigenous professionals working, and student participating, in higher education. (NASPA, 2010)

ACPA's Native American Network is part of a broader group called the Standing Committee for Multicultural Affairs (CMA), which includes individual networks representing the Asian Pacific American, Latino, multi-racial, and Pan African communities. The published mission and goals of the CMA are as follows:

> Mission: The mission of CMA is to focus attention on, and educate the student affairs profession about, the issues and concerns of people of color in higher education.
>
> Goals: The goal of CMA is to act as the coordinating directorate body for diversity initiatives among the different CMA networks. CMA actively seeks to promote the recognition and celebration of all students, staff, and faculty of color in higher education by serving as an advocacy committee within ACPA. (ACPA, 2010)

Prior to the formation of NANIPKC, the fledgling field of Native American student affairs was, as it continues to be, supported by the National Institute for Native Leadership in Higher Education (NINLHE, pronounced nin-lee), founded in 1993. Originally formed to support Native American student retention programs and their directors, NINLHE has grown to include Native higher education leaders and allies who work to support the success of Native American college students. NINLHE's stated mission is

> to transform higher education in the United States and Canada in ways that improve the experiences and educational outcomes of Native students, which includes Native American, Alaska Native, Native Hawaiian, and Aboriginal peoples.
>
> NINLHE works to enhance the professional skills and bolster resilience of higher education professionals, both Native and non-Native, responsible for improving Native student recruitment, retention and graduation rates. By strengthening the capacity of these individuals, who are essential for Native student success, and promoting culturally appropriate practices, NINLHE improves the educational training experience of Native students as well as the professional environment for staff and faculty across the United States and Canada. As a peer among other professional associations, NINLHE will use our collective expertise and influence to provide leadership to the national higher education community. (NIN-LHE, 2010)

In addition to the student affairs–focused associations and organizations, two other major organizations support Native Americans in higher education: the National Indian Education Association (NIEA) and the American

Indian Higher Education Consortium (AIHEC). The NIEA reports that it is the oldest (founded in 1970) and largest Indian education organization committed to increasing educational opportunities and resources for American Indian, Alaska Native, and Native Hawaiian students and protecting cultural and linguistic traditions in the United States. The purpose of the NIEA is to promote educational equity, and it is focused primarily on pre-kindergarten through high school education. However, higher education is increasingly represented among NIEA members as stronger ties are developed between secondary and postsecondary educational systems, including tribal colleges and universities (TCUs). AIHEC was founded in 1972 by the presidents of the first six tribal colleges as an informal collaboration among member colleges (AIHEC, 2010). AIHEC has grown, along with the number of TCUs, to over 30 membership institutions. Other national organizations, such as the National Education Association (NEA) and the College Board, support active interest groups for and with Native Americans.

With the NIEA representing itself as the oldest national Indian education organization in the United States, even among Native groups in student affairs national associations, it may be surprising to learn that Native Americans remain a relatively new phenomenon in the Euro-American construct of national associations and organizations, while simultaneously being the original inhabitants of this continent. This raises important considerations when thinking about the role and function of Native Americans, both within Native and non-Native national associations and organizations.

A recent in-depth study by student affairs professionals exploring the social construction of Native American college students found that student affairs professionals often hold deficit views of Native Americans that translate into their broader professional thinking (McClellan, 2003). In fact, McClellan (2003) found that "Native Americans and other groups with small participation rates are marginalized in student affairs and within the socialization of student affairs professionals . . . the profession is not fully democratized and as such may not be able to provide the best possible support for the democratization of higher education" (p. 204).

Part of this process includes the "othering" of Native Americans within higher education multicultural professional frameworks and, subsequently, in professional circles. This experience is often similar to the marginalization experienced by Native American students on college campuses (Garland, 2007, 2010; Lowe 2005).

The structures of national associations often replicate the hierarchical nature of higher education institutions themselves, thereby limiting the organizational voices of small populations such as Native Americans (Garland,

2010). Further, some organizations, such as ACPA's Native American Network, may find themselves situated so deep within an association's organizational framework that raising issues facing Native Americans (professionals or students) is difficult, at best, often requiring member resources that burden an already small population. While not necessarily intentional on the part of ACPA's governing board, this traditional structure of placing all small populations within a single "multicultural" constituent group does not effectively support the ideals of shared governance that many higher education associations, including ACPA, espouse. Tierney (2008) proposes that one of the processes of shared governance among organizations includes opportunities for operationalizing beliefs members hold as important that are often reflected in the group's visions and mission. As McClellan (2003) discusses, this type of democratization is difficult for an already small population of people to achieve with what Tierney describes as a reinterpretation of the organization as new participants bring with them a new understanding of the organization's values and purpose. When this does not happen, the resulting status quo often privileges majority groups over groups with fewer.

Overcoming Structural and Organizational Barriers of Participation

As most national organizations are a reflection of U.S. IHEs, it stands to reason that, since the majority of colleges and universities are predominantly White in their student, staff, and faculty makeup, the reflective national organizations share similar representations. Many of the historical, organizational, and structural barriers for participation by non-White members in organizations with long histories do not escape those associations affiliated with higher education, including student affairs. As mentioned earlier, many national associations were products of racial and gender segregation systems in higher education. As such, predominantly White institutions (PWIs) of higher education often shared in a disproportionate distribution of resources (e.g., state support of public schools, students whose families could afford tuition), which ultimately benefited the organizations to which the universities and its faculty and staff belonged.

To their credit, several national associations, including those in student affairs, were early advocates of a civil rights and social justice ethos in the United States, even when many individual institutions struggled to be open for all students. However, as Tierney (2008) points out, context matters in colleges and organizations proclaiming an ethos of social justice and shared governance. As we have seen with the compartmentalization of multiculturalism within colleges and higher education associations, shared governance actions may not be living up to member expectations, especially for those whose psychosocial membership is represented by a multicultural perspective. In other words, unless the majority of members in an organization understand the unique structural and organizational barriers to full organizational participation by *all* its members, especially those from historically small and marginalized populations, the organization will never achieve the social justice, equity, and inclusive ethos it envisions.

ACPA and NASPA have made great strides over the past decade to acknowledge Native Americans in both higher education and their membership. However, acknowledgment is only a first step. ACPA and NASPA publish two of the field's primary research journals as well as books and other publications disseminating knowledge about student development and practice. One area in which Native Americans continue to be invisible, and what this book is helping to address, includes printed material by, about, or with Native American college students and student affairs professionals. Compared with the research and publications of primary racial and ethnic groups, Native Americans continue to be invisible. Since the overall American Indian population is likely to maintain its steady 1% proportion of the U.S. population for the near future, this population's quantitative representation will likely remain an ongoing challenge, not only in research data, but also in an association's visible representation.

In the United States, an individual is often grouped by others into a phenotypically associated racial/ethnic category. This crude way of identifying others is often used for anecdotal data gathering, such as program participation and attendance rates by people of color. Owing to the widely diverse phenotypes of North American Indians, visual racial/ethnic grouping and identification by others is often complicated and ambiguous. Additionally, many Native Americans may have mixed ancestry, from either other tribes or racial/ethnic groups. An association may not identify Native Americans visually within their groupings of professionals as easily as it does other racial/ethnic groups, thereby contributing to an overall sense of Native American invisibility. Moving beyond visual recognition of differences, especially when considering race/ethnicity, is an important step for associations to take on their paths to cultural competence.

Further, the increased use of multiracial demographic categories on membership forms that do not allow for a specific subset of racial identification(s) may mask an already small population of Native Americans within an organization, and even on campus. Native Americans, as well as many African Americans, have been wrestling with multiracial identities since colonization. For Native Americans, early federal policy provided plans to lighten the skin of Native Americans through intermarrying so they would assimilate into Euro-American culture and eventually be seen by others as White (Takaki, 1993). As we know, this experiment failed, and Native American and tribal identity is experiencing a resurgence thanks to sovereignty movements over the past century. So someone who may mark "multiracial" on a demographic form, may also choose (if available) to list his or her primary racial identity as Native American. With many Native Americans coming from multiracial backgrounds, the absence of what constitutes their "multiracialness" is likely to provide an inaccurate snapshot of an association's racial/ethnic membership when considering Native American members. As current U.S. culture, including today's college students, wrestles with the increasing use of a multiracial identity, Native American members can provide subtle insight into the positive outcomes and pitfalls of a multiracial demographic, especially when the population accounts for less than 1% of an organization's membership.

It should always be remembered that Native Americans are not a monolithic group. In fact, they represent one or more of the more than 500 tribes in North America today. Each tribe often has unique heritage and customs as well as its own language. As mentioned earlier, Native Americans within organizations are frequently expected to represent themselves as part of a Native or Indigenous group without regard to their within-group differences. However, one similarity that many tribal members of associations seem to share is a desire to work together through consensus within what is often a complex and hierarchically driven organization that frequently minimizes small-population voices.

Speaking about the ongoing struggle for understanding between the Indigenous and non-Indigenous people of North America, Paul Chaat Smith (2009) writes,

> And for the [non-Indigenous] Americans, who drive Pontiacs and Cherokees and live in places with Indian names, like Manhattan and Chicago and Idaho, we [Native Americans] remain a half-remembered presence, both comforting and dangerous, lurking just below the surface. We are hopelessly fascinated with each other, locked in an endless embrace of love and hate and narcissism. Together we are condemned forever to disappoint, never to forget even as we can't remember. Our snapshots and home

movies create an American epic. It is fate, destiny. And why not?, We are the country, and the country is us. (p. 6)

Future Directions for National Student Affairs Associations With Native American Members

This chapter has identified several ideas and practical applications for national associations to consider when involving, working with, and engaging their Native American members. This section pulls these ideas and applications together and proposes a few more that may help ensure that Native American members are visible and their voices heard.

Native American participation in student affairs associations may be predicated on their participation as college students. As we know, Native American students are the most likely group not to attend college, and of those attending, the most likely not to complete college in six years (NCES, 2009). Therefore, it stands to reason that Native American representation in the student affairs profession will be an ongoing struggle, as it is for almost all professions. Further, this requires all of higher education to focus not only on increasing Native American college student participation and success in college, but also on mentoring and fostering new professionals. Both ACPA and NASPA have active next-generation (of student affairs) groups and should intentionally reach out to ensure Native American participation. In the meantime, it should be an ongoing responsibility for national associations to build ally groups that promote Native American participation and leadership in our associations.

National associations, as organizations, should become more active in supporting Native American higher education, and Native American student affairs, more specifically. Until now, the specific area of Native American student affairs has been left to the small groups of Native American members who are often entry- and mid-level practitioners and are not represented in senior student affairs positions. With a lack of Native Americans in high-level positions, few institutional and organizational resources are directed toward Native American member needs and organizational support. Greater numbers of culturally competent Native American allies are necessary if our associations are to become multicultural organizations that include Native Americans.

Our national associations and their leaders must become more confident as listeners and allies, rather than anxious and reactionary, when it comes to

Native American ways of organizational engagement. There is often a disconnect between organizational loyalty to the previously discussed Euro-American organizational structure and Indigenous approaches to communication and decision making. In fact, hierarchy and cultural missteps are both easily managed by culturally competent well-meaning professionals. This leads us to identify who are our Native American members in associations. As discovered in preparing this chapter, ACPA allows for only a single mark in the race/ethnicity category when a member registers. And many Native Americans are of mixed racial ancestry, so they may mark the multiracial category. Without an option to mark the Native American category as well, associations may be participating inadvertently in demographic assimilation of Native American members, which results in an inaccurate portrayal of their Native American membership, thereby contributing to invisibility.

Our national associations are also responsible for the development and dissemination of knowledge in our field. Native Americans have historically been invisible in our research and student development literature, and this must not be allowed to continue. Recently ACPA and NASPA have recognized this problem, primarily owing to the activism of their Native American members, and they are becoming more intentional with their inclusion of Native American college student research and knowledge dissemination. While this is a recent positive development, there is much ground to make up when comparing our knowledge of Native Americans with that of other college students. Mentoring more Native American researchers and writers is an obvious remedy, but so is the way research is carried out. It is no longer acceptable, or ethical in the view of this chapter's authors, to leave Native Americans out of research studies in which student data are examined across race/ethnicity. The national associations should develop research protocols for assisting their member researchers and practitioners to understand this phenomenon and how to become more inclusive in our field's knowledge acquisition and dissemination.

Student affairs national associations should reach out through their own members to other Native American groups and associations for ongoing collaborations and projects. These partnerships may result in increased cultural competence activities for members of all participating associations. The within-group diversity among Native American student affairs professionals brings unique and deep understandings that, when included intentionally, will help our associations become the true multicultural associations they aspire to be.

References

American College Personnel Association. (2010). Constitution and bylaws. Available from ww2.myacpa.org/cma-home/constitution

American College Personnel Association. (2011). [Numbers]. Unpublished raw data.

American Indian Higher Education Consortium (AIHEC). (2010). AIHEC's history and mission. Retrieved from http://www.aihec.org/about/historyMission.cfm

Evans, N. J., & Williams, T. E. (1998). Student affairs faculty: Characteristics, qualifications, and recommendations for future preparation. In N. J. Evans & C. E. Phelps (Eds.), *The state of the art of preparation and practice in student affairs* (pp. 105–123). Washington, DC: American College Personnel Association.

Garland, J. L. (2007). [Review of the book *Serving Native American Students: New Directions for Student Services*]. *Journal of College Student Development, 48,* 612–614.

Garland, J. L. (2010). Removing the college involvement "research asterisk": Identifying and rethinking predictors of American Indian college student involvement. Doctoral dissertation. Retrieved from http://hdl.handle.net/1903/10781

Hunter, D. E., & Beeler, K. J. (1991). Through the "looking glass" at preparation needed for student affairs research. In K. J. Beer & D. E. Hunter (Eds.), *Puzzles and pieces in wonderland: The promise and practice of student affairs research* (pp. 106–123). San Francisco: Jossey-Bass.

Hunter, D. E., & Comey, D. (1991). Common learning in student affairs. *NASPA Journal, 29,* 10–16.

Lowe, S. C. (2005). This is who I am: Experience of Native American students. In M. J. Tippeconnic Fox, S. C. Lowe, & G. S. McClellan (Eds.), *Serving Native American students* (New Direction for Student Services No. 109, pp. 33–40). San Francisco: Jossey-Bass.

McClellan, G. S. (2003). Multiculturalism as a "Technology of Othering": An exploratory study of the social construction of Native Americans by student affairs professionals in the southwest. Doctoral dissertation. Retrieved from ProQuest Digital Dissertation database (AAT AAT3089979)

McEwen, M. K., Williams, T. E., & Engstrom, C. M. (1991). Feminization in student affairs: A qualitative investigation. *Journal of College Student Development, 32,* 440–446.

Moore, L. V., & Neuberger, C. G. (1998). How professional associations are addressing issues in student affairs. In N. J. Evans, & C. E. Phelps Tobin (Eds.), *The state of the art of preparation and practice in student affairs: Another look* (pp. 61–80). Lanham, MD: American College Personnel Association.

National Association for Student Personnel Administrators (NASPA). (1987). A perspective on student affairs. Retrieved from http://www.naspa.org/pubs/his.cfm

National Association for Student Personnel Administrators (NASPA). (2010). Knowledge Community: Indigenous Peoples. Retrieved from http://www.naspa.org/kc/ipkc/default.cfm

National Center for Education Statistics. (2009). *Integrated postsecondary education data system.* Retrieved July 29, 2009, from http://nces.ed.gov/IPEDS/about/

National Institute for Native Leadership in Higher Education. (2010). Retrieved from http://ninlhe.unm.edu/

Nuss, E. M. (1996). The development of student affairs. In S. R. Komives & D. B. Woodard Jr. (Eds.), *Student services: A handbook for the profession* (3rd ed., pp. 22–43). San Francisco: Jossey-Bass.

Nuss, E. M. (2000). The role of professional associations. In M. J. Barr & M. K. Desler (Eds.), *The handbook of student affairs administration* (2nd ed., pp. 492–507). San Francisco: Jossey-Bass.

Nuss, E .M. (2003). The development of student affairs. In S. R. Komives & D. B. Woodard, Jr. (Eds.), *Student services: A handbook for the profession* (4th ed., pp. 65–88). San Francisco: Jossey-Bass.

Pope, R. L., Reynolds, A. L., & Cheatham, H. E. (1997). American College Personnel Association's strategic initiative on multiculturalism: A report and proposal. *Journal of College Student Development, 38,* 62–67.

Schrank, M., & Young, R. B. (1987, Spring). The role of professional associations. *New Directions for Student Services, 37,* 61–68.

Smith, P. C. (2009). *Everything you know about Indians is wrong.* Minneapolis: University of Minnesota Press.

Takaki, R. (1993). *A different mirror—A history of multicultural America.* Toronto, Canada: Little, Brown, and Company.

Tierney, W. G. (1992). *Official encouragement, unofficial discouragement: Minorities in academe—the American Indian experience.* Norwood, NJ: Ablex.

Woodard, D. B., Jr., Love, P. L., & Komives, S. R. (2000). *Leadership and management issues for a new century* (New Directions for Student Services, No. 92). San Francisco: Jossey-Bass.

CONCLUSION

Dr. Stephanie J. Waterman (Onondaga, Turtle), Dr. Heather J. Shotton (Wichita/Kiowa/Cheyenne), Shelly C. Lowe (Diné), Dr. Donna Brown (Turtle Mountain Chippewa)

Through the efforts of our colleagues invested in Native American college students, this book has added to the knowledge so often dismissed behind an asterisk. Chapters were written by Native American student affairs practitioners, faculty members, and non-Native allies, *all of our relations*, who are on the ground, in the trenches, working with our students every day. It is hard, good work, and we thank them for their dedication.

Our book began with chapters that focused on student experiences and student support, such as the University of Arizona's First-Year Scholars Program and the new historically Native American fraternity and sorority movement. Chapters on administrative matters, such as collaborating with TCUs, the role of professional organizations, and role models, followed. An underlying conceptual framework throughout these chapters is the importance of using Indigenous epistemology and knowledge systems when working with Native students and communities.

Indigenous pedagogies are based on our relationships with each other, our communities, the land, the animals, and everything on Mother Earth, including the cosmos. Our responsibility to these relationships and the reciprocity among all parties helps us make meaning of our surroundings. These relationships also assist us in defining who we are (Deloria & Wildcat, 2001). "Everything is alive and aware, requiring that relationships be maintained in a respectful way so as not to upset the balance" (Kawagley & Barnhardt, 1999, p. 127). Knowledge is spiritual and sacred (Deloria & Wildcat, 2001). Moreover, because we are a politicized people, Indigenous pedagogies are "inherently political" (Grande, 2008, p. 250). By saying, "this is my experience," "this is how I understand," "this is my peoples' understanding," we are enacting our sovereignty. Indigenous knowledge systems value observation and personal experience. "In other words, individuals live and enact their knowledge and, in the process, engage further in the process of coming to be—of forming a way of engaging others and the world" (Brayboy & Maughan, 2009, p. 4).

This underlying Indigenous knowledge system was overtly explicit in Martin and Thunder's chapter, "Incorporating Native Culture into Student Affairs." The authors began with their personal, yet collective experience of formal education. Their blending of an Indigenous tradition with a Western education to become the dedicated practitioners and educators they are today was written in a spiritual way. Martin and Thunder showed us the importance of spirituality and how to incorporate an Indigenous framework into programming within non-Native, Western environments. They explained so eloquently Indigenous ways "of coming to be" (Brayboy & Maughan, 2009, p. 4). While the other chapters also use this framework, what is critical in each one is that this is *our* voice and *our* experiences. As editors we respect each author's knowledge, honor each author's perspectives, and allow each of them to lead the way.

Throughout this book the authors have provided valuable insight into our understanding of working with Native students, bringing to the forefront critical issues and knowledge about this population. More important, they have made tangible recommendations for how to better serve Native students at NNCUs. Based on their insight, we offer broad recommendations for graduate students, student affairs professionals, and administrators at all levels.

Challenge Yourself to Look Beyond the Asterisk

Too often the literature and recommendations presented in courses and workshops and at conferences and summits omit, or fail to include, information and recommendations on the experiences of, or how to work with, Native American students, simply because data on this population are not statistically significant. Even though this may be the case, it is a good idea to ask and speculate about what would be presented if the data were available. More important, ask yourself why these data are excluded, and why this practice has become acceptable to so many. Who is being served by excluding Native Americans from the higher education dialogue? How is this a disservice to our students and our campuses? Challenge yourself to look beyond the asterisk rhetoric, ask questions, and start a dialogue. There may be fellow classmates, coworkers, faculty, or professionals with some knowledge and experience who can share their insight and help move the conversation forward.

Get to Know the Tribal Groups in Your Area

Take it upon yourself to learn more about Native people, particularly the tribes in the region in which you work. Native students are most likely to attend college near their homes and families, so the majority of your students probably will be from the closest Indian reservation or Native community. Understand that Native community is defined in several ways and is present in various places: reservations, rural areas, and urban areas alike. Take the time to visit the tribal areas near your institution, introduce yourself, and participate in public tribal events. If your institution is located near a major urban area, get to know the urban Native community. There are large pockets of Native communities in urban areas (e.g., Chicago, Los Angeles, New York City, Minneapolis, and Oklahoma City), many of which have community centers that are gathering places for the Native community. Take time to learn about these communities.

Learn about the contemporary issues of importance to these communities and offer to give presentations so they can become aware of the work your office does, the services your institution provides, or the research you are conducting; reach out to your surrounding Native communities. In addition, be sure to know the history of your institution, especially as it relates to tribal affairs in the state, region, or nation. Does your institutional mission continue to address this history, and what is your office's role in supporting the institutional mission as it relates to Native Americans?

Know Your Institutional Resources

Be aware of the Native American resources on your campus. Is there a Native American Student Support Service Unit, and, if so, with what programs and offices does this unit partner? What services does your institution provide for Native students? What are the strengths of your university in relation to Native American Studies, outreach, and research? Many institutions are leaders in specific fields, and tribes seek them out for support and expertise in tackling some of their most challenging issues. Many institutions have a dedicated staff member such as an advisor on Native American affairs or a dedicated program whose directive is to coordinate with tribal communities. Other institutions have active memorandums of understanding with tribal programs, tribal colleges, or tribal communities. Know whom to ask when questions about such things come up, or when your office/program has questions of its own. Experts at your institution may be Native or non-Native, but the most important factor is knowledge and experience.

Assume Tribal Diversity

Even though the tribal groups in your region may all be related and similar in cultural representation, the Native American students at your institution are more than likely from varying tribal backgrounds. They may come from reservation areas and have strong ties to their tribal culture, they may come from urban areas and have little knowledge of their Native heritage, and many of them will lie somewhere in between. Assuming there is one Native culture and one way to include Native American culture in programming and events could be offensive to this diverse population, and this assumption could isolate some Native students. It is important to understand that each Native student brings his or her own unique tribal histories, experiences, and identity.

Be sure to work with a wide range of Native American students when planning events and programs to ensure that you are not generalizing to one tribal group. Because of the great diversity and variation among Native people, it is difficult to describe a set of values that encompasses all groups, so programming and events should not address a single set of values or cultural representations unless this is the intended focus. Additionally, create and take advantage of advisory groups made up of various university personnel, faculty, and local tribal community members. It might be very appropriate to create programming and support events that are specific to the local tribal culture, but it is also appropriate to support events focused on others. An advisory group can help identify programming and events or speakers/groups that are inappropriate or are misrepresentative.

Be Aware of Negative Imagery

How does your institution relate to Native mascots, logos, nicknames, and other imagery used by colleges and universities? All student affairs professionals should have some knowledge of the history of the use of Native imagery and the implications and consequences of this imagery on Native students. Has a fraternity on your campus promoted a social event by degrading and sexualizing Native American men or women? Even if you are not aware of instances such as this, it is likely Native American students on your campus are very aware of such instances if they have occurred, and they will expect an institutional response. Find out how other universities and administrators have addressed such situations successfully and plan to tackle such instances on your campus immediately.

Assess Campus Climate

Does your campus have visible Native faculty and staff, or a space for students just to hang out? Does your institution approach Native communities and research in a respectful way? Are staff trained and willing to work with Native communities that may operate on a different calendar? If a Native student experiences an act of racism, are there procedures in place to assist the student? Are there policies in place to deal with racism for *any* student? Are you sure Native students feel they can engage in that system? Native mascots, campus parties that involve "red face" (the Native equivalent of Black face), and institutional research on reservations without benefit to the community are only a few ways in which campus climate can be negatively affected. In environments with Native mascots, it may be difficult for non-Native personnel to recognize this as racism. It is important for the campus to be a welcoming place, and conducting an assessment of campus climate will benefit both students and the institution. It is important, though, to be sure the assessment is culturally appropriate.

Cultural Competency and Self-Assessment

Cultural competency should be addressed and assessed throughout student affairs programs. Cultural competence is commonly misunderstood as knowing everything there is to know about a certain culture to serve people of that culture competently. Sue and Sue (2008) define a *culturally competent professional* as one who is in the process of actively developing and practicing appropriate, relevant, and sensitive intervention strategies and skills in working with his or her culturally different client. There are three competency goals associated with this definition.

The first competency is awareness of one's own assumptions, values, and biases. A culturally competent professional is one who is actively in the process of becoming aware of his or her own assumptions about human behavior, values, biases, preconceived notions, personal limitations, and so forth. Examination of the self is difficult because of the emotional impact brought on by examining one's own attitudes, beliefs, and feelings associated with cultural differences, such as racism, sexism, and heterosexism.

The second competency is actively attempting to understand the world-view of the culturally diverse. A culturally competent professional must be able to understand and share the worldview of others. This does not mean one must hold these worldviews as his or her own, but that the professional can see and accept other views in a nonjudgmental manner. Recognize and validate the experiences of Native American students. It is less controversial and more comfortable for student affairs professionals to reason away feelings of oppression, racism, and hate. It is very important to accept as fact the perceptions and worldview of Native students, staff, faculty, and administrators.

The third competency is actively developing appropriate intervention strategies and techniques. Student affairs professionals develop their best strategies for recruitment and retention when they consider the life experiences and cultural values of their students. This is to say, programming that works with other racial/underrepresented student populations may not be appropriate for Native students. Furthermore, programming and interventions may need to be adjusted for students from different tribes, rural and urban upbringings, different socioeconomic backgrounds, and so forth.

Practicum and Internship Placement

Fulfilling a practicum and/or internship requirement in a Native student services office, or a multicultural affairs office, can provide a rich and comprehensive experience for the graduate student enrolled in a student affairs program. Most of these offices are responsible for a broad array of functions, including recruitment, retention, and alumni relations. Recruitment can include school visits and follow-up, hosting groups on campus, and assisting prospective students in the admissions and financial aid application processes. Retention services cover a broad array of services, including housing, financial aid, advising, tutoring, and advocacy. Alumni relations can include tracking graduates, producing an alumni newsletter, and hosting alumni events.

Native communities, urban and tribal, may also benefit from the availability of an intern. Communities may need tutors or media and communication assistance, for example. Many urban centers work with the elderly and have child care services. Does the center need accounting assistance, computer expertise? Does it have mountains of documents to be read, scanned, or organized? Native communities are also often engaged in environmental issues, including fish and wildlife management. Contact these communities to see whether there are any opportunities that are beneficial to students, the institution, and/or the community.

Also consider the benefits of fulfilling a practicum and/or internship experience at a tribal college. Owing in part to the relatively small size of the college, the student potentially could be supervised by a high-level administrator, such as the dean of students, the vice president for student services, or even the president. The student would likely not be confined to one department, but could spend time in a variety of offices, providing extra help during times of peak activity. For example, a single internship could involve placement in the financial aid office during aid packaging, assisting with orientation and registration in the first few weeks of classes, and tutoring and academic support during the semester. Probably the most valuable part of the internship would be the opportunity to experience cultural immersion throughout all areas of the college attributable to the unique nature of incorporating culture and language in all aspects of the tribal college experience.

Increasing Native American Presence

Native professionals should have a presence throughout campus. While they do play crucial roles in Native American Student Services Units (NASSUs) or multicultural student affairs offices, they should not be confined to these areas alone. It is beneficial for Native students to have allies in many departments on campus, and expertise gained in much-needed student support offices, such as admissions, financial aid, career placement, or commuter affairs, can be shared with tribal communities to help prepare incoming Native students. In addition, the personal experience and outlook of a Native American staff member can enhance and inform all staff. The expertise that a Native staff member gains will also extend beyond the position and into the larger tribal community.

Having a Place to Be

Throughout this book, the authors discussed the importance of having a place on campus to be, to feel safe, and to connect with other Native students, faculty, and staff. This is clear in Ecklund and Terrance's chapter,

"Extending the Rafters: Cultural Context for Native American Students," and Tachine and Francis-Begay's chapter, "First-Year Experience for Native American Freshmen: The University of Arizona First-Year Scholars Program." However, a place to be and a place "to come to be" (Brayboy & Maughan, 2009, p. 4) undergird all the chapters. In a colonized land, where institutions of higher education are reminders of removal, the residential school era, and a hegemonic curriculum, a physical place to feel safe is critical. Native students report experiencing microaggression from other students, staff, and faculty (Brayboy, Fann, Castagno, & Solyom, 2012). But on a larger level, this land is Native land, now occupied mostly by non-Natives; an office, a floor in a residence hall, or a building acknowledges the original people of this land and is a meaningful and respectful act. Advocate for space on your campus.

Recommendations

We conclude with an overview of themes from the chapter recommendations. When working with students and Native communities, remember that it takes time to build trust. Be willing to learn and listen. Be open to our spirituality and be aware that students may not share details of their spirituality. As was evident in chapter 2, many Native people combine church with Indigenous spirituality. Be open to our definition of family and welcome them, even if that means that one student may have more than 13 people show up for a campus family event. Try to be holistic in your programming to support the whole student. Remember, students are our priority.

There are many policies in place that may deter our students or produce an unwelcoming climate. Examine your institution's policies. If your campus has a Native American mascot, be aware that the mascot may not be perceived as welcoming. Other policies that might affect Native students negatively can be tied to funding and resource support. For example, even though historically Native American fraternities and sororities have incorporated Native culture to fill a gap in student support, they are still subject to campus and national organizational policies that hinder growth. For example, a Native Greek organization must fulfill the same campus regulations (such as insurance and fees) as an organization 10 times its size with 10 times the resources and members. Also, expansion of Greek organizations is often referred to as *colonization*, a term that is highly problematic for Native people. Colonization of the Americas nearly exterminated the Indigenous people, setting in motion a highly violent period from which we are still recovering. Reconsider common language and institutional culture that may marginalize Native students.

Being flexible is another recommendation. Individual nations operate on their own calendars and spiritual terms. This means non-Native leaders may have to wait or change plans because a spiritual or community need comes before a campus need. Clear communication is extremely important and part of building trust with students and with communities. It is also imperative that student affairs personnel educate themselves about the experiences of Native students and the Native communities they serve as well as provide support to their staff and coworkers so they can also learn more.

This means higher education personnel must do some homework. First, they must build and maintain relationships. Find trusted personnel on the campus and in the community. To be inclusive and transformative means inviting us to the table beyond Native American month and when a Native American issue is in the news. Invite us to the table when discussing hiring—at all levels—curriculum planning, financial aid, art installations, diversity, and so on.

Above all, it is important to be holistic in our support of students. Their well-being is more than retention and academics. We want our students, our future leaders, to be healthy mentally, spiritually, and physically; happy would be good, too. As student affairs professionals and educators, we all know how difficult it can be to balance our work, our families and communities, our spirituality, and our academics. We need to be good role models for our students and our coworkers. We do neither our students nor our profession any good if we overwork ourselves. Just as we have answered a call to continue the conversation on Natives in higher education and to support avenues to move beyond the asterisk phenomenon, we as Native professionals in higher education have first and foremost answered the call to bring our students to our campuses, support them, celebrate with them when they succeed, and return them home or send them out to the larger world as leaders and voices of our future. Our book addresses the complicated ways in which we interact with higher education to expose the richness beyond the asterisk.

We close with words from one of our elders, Dr. Henrietta Mann, Cheyenne. We urge you to remember these words as you work with our students, communities, and coworkers. The concept of "walking in two worlds," Native and non-Native, has been described by many, but Dr. Mann said she saw herself as Cheyenne no matter where she was. It was the only way she knew to view and interpret the world and her place in it.

Finally, we wish to thank those who went before us, and Creation for making this book possible.

We are finished, *da netoh*, and thank you, it is good: *ahe'hee', ah-ho day-own-day*, and *nya weñha*.

References

Brayboy, B. M. J., Fann, A. J., Castagno, A. E., & Solyom, J. A. (2012). Postsecondary education for American Indian and Alaska Natives: Higher education for nation building and self-determination. *ASHE Higher Education Report, 37*(5), 1–154. doi: 10.1002/aehe.3705

Brayboy, B. M. J., & Maughan, E. (2009). Indigenous knowledges and the story of the bean. *Harvard Educational Review, 79*(1), 1–21.

Deloria, V., Jr., & Wildcat, D. R. (2001). *Power and place: Indian education in America.* Golden, CO: Fulcrum.

Grande, S. (2008). Red pedagogy: The un-methodology. In N. K. Denzin, Y. S. Lincoln, & L. T. Smith (Eds.), *Handbook of critical and indigenous methodologies.* (pp. 233–254). Los Angeles: Sage.

Kawagley, A. O., & Barnhardt, R. (1999). Education indigenous to place: Western science meets Native reality. In G. A. Smith & D. R. Williams (Eds.), *Ecological education in action: On weaving education, culture, and the environment* (pp. 117–140). Albany: State University of New York Press.

Sue, D. W., & Sue, D. (2008). *Counseling the culturally diverse: Theory and practice* (5th ed.). Hoboken, NJ: Wiley & Sons.

ABOUT THE EDITORS AND CONTRIBUTORS

Editors

Dr. Heather J. Shotton is a member of the Wichita & Affiliated Tribes, and is also of Kiowa and Cheyenne descent. She currently serves as an assistant professor in Native American studies at the University of Oklahoma. Dr. Shotton has worked in the field of higher education serving Native American students for several years, in both academics and student services.

Shelly C. Lowe is Diné from Ganado, Arizona. She is the executive director of the Harvard University Native American Program (HUNAP). She previously worked in Native American student affairs at Yale University and in American Indian Studies at The University of Arizona.

Dr. Stephanie J. Waterman is Onondaga, Turtle Clan. She is an assistant professor in Higher Education administration in Educational Leadership at the Warner Graduate School of Education and Human Development, University of Rochester, having previously served as the faculty associate for the Syracuse University Native Student Program.

Contributors

Dr. Donna Brown (Turtle Mountain Chippewa) is assistant professor and coordinator of Student Affairs Program at Minnesota State University–Moorhead.

Dr. Charlotte E. Davidson (Diné/Mandan, Hidatsa and Arikara) is a faculty member at the University of Illinois, Urbana-Champagne.

CHiXapkaid (Dr. D. Michael Pavel) (Skokomish) is professor of education studies at the University of Oregon.

Dr. Timothy Ecklund is associate vice president for Campus Life at Buffalo State College.

Karen Francis-Begay (Diné) is special advisor to the president at The University of Arizona.

Dr. John L. Garland (Choctaw) is assistant professor at the Rehabilitation Counseling Program at the University of Alabama.

Dr. Justin Guillory (Nez Perce Descendant) is dean of Academics and Distance Learning at Northwest Indian College.

Freida Jacques (Onondaga)

Steven C. Martin (Muscogee Creek) is director of the Native American Student Center at the University of Idaho.

Dr. George S. McClellan is vice chancellor for Student Affairs at Indiana University–Purdue University Fort Wayne.

Dr. Robin Minthorn (Kiowa/Nez Perce/Apache/ Assiniboine/Umatilla) is coordinator of Native American Affairs at Oklahoma State University.

Derek Oxendine (Lumbee) is director of the Office of Native American Student Affairs at North Carolina State University.

Symphony Oxendine (Cherokee/Mississippi Choctaw) is a doctoral student at the University of North Carolina at Greensboro.

Dr. Cornel Pewewardy (Comanche/Kiowa) is director of the Native American Studies Program at Portland State University.

Molly Springer (Cherokee Nation of Oklahoma) is director of the Dartmouth College Native American Program.

Amanda Tachine (Diné) is a doctoral student in Higher Education at The University of Arizona.

Danielle Terrance (Mohawk) is a doctoral candidate at The Ohio State University.

Adrienne L. Thunder (Ho-Chunk) is executive director of the Ho-Chunk Nation Department of Education.

INDEX

AAIP. *See* Association of American Indian
Physicians
AASA. *See* African American Student Affairs
access
as collaboration benefit, 98–99
college access and first-year retention
factors, 26–28
ACPA. *See* American College Personnel
Association
ACT, 136
ACUHO-I. *See* Association of College and
University Housing Officials
International
ADVANCE Purdue, 119
AFA. *See* Association of Fraternity/Sorority
Advisors
African Americans. *See also* Black
fraternalism
culture, 55
programs for, 110–11
African American Student Affairs (AASA),
29
AIA. *See* American Indian Alumni
AIAC. *See* American Indian Advisory
Council
AIANNHP. *See* American Indian, Alaska
Native and Native Hawaiian Program
AICAE. *See* American Indian Council of
Architects and Engineers
AIGC. *See* American Indian Graduate
Center
AIHEC. *See* American Indian Higher
Education Consortium
AILDI. *See* American Indian Language
Development Institute
AIP. *See* American Indian Program
AIRO. *See* American Indian Research
Opportunities

AIS. *See* American Indian Studies
AISC. *See* American Indian Studies Center
AISES. *See* American Indian Science and
Engineering Society
AISS. *See* American Indian Student Services
Akwe:kon (residential house), 58, 59, 118
Allen, W., 70
Alpha Phi Alpha Fraternity, Inc., 68
Alpha Pi Omega, 68, 75
alumni relations, 170
American College Personnel Association
(ACPA), 64, 152–54, 159, 161–62. *See
also* Native American Network
American Indian, 4, 85
American Indian, Alaska Native and Native
Hawaiian Program (AIANNHP), 116
American Indian Advisory Council (AIAC),
85
American Indian/Alaska Native Religious
Freedom Act (1978), 116
American Indian Alumni (AIA), 84
American Indian Council of Architects and
Engineers (AICAE), 132
American Indian Graduate Center (AIGC),
61, 131
American Indian Higher Education
Consortium (AIHEC), 131, 156–57
American Indian Language Development
Institute (AILDI), 83
American Indian Program (AIP), 58–59, 111,
118
American Indian research asterisk, 2
American Indian Research Opportunities
(AIRO), 101
American Indian Science and Engineering
Society (AISES), 117, 131
American Indian Student Services (AISS),
116

Also available from Stylus

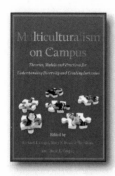

Multiculturalism on Campus
Theory, Models, and Practices for Understanding Diversity and Creating Inclusion
Edited by Michael J. Cuyjet, Mary F. Howard-Hamilton, and
Diane L. Cooper

"An excellent resourceful book that faculty and administrators can use to enhance multiculturalism on college campuses."—*Journal of College Student Development*

"Offers suggestions for creating an inclusive environment for underrepresented groups."—*The Chronicle of Higher Education*

"In two words: impressively comprehensive. New professionals and seasoned administrators alike will find much that is useful in this book. The editors have assembled a dynamic constellation of scholars who offer rich insights into the texture and substance of multiculturalism on contemporary college campuses. Anyone who aspires to become a more culturally competent and responsive educator should read this text."—**Shaun R. Harper,** *Graduate School of Education, Africana Studies and Gender Studies, The University of Pennsylvania*

Ethnicity in College
Advancing Theory and Improving Diversity Practices on Campus
Anna M. Ortiz, and Silvia J. Santos

"Ortiz and Santos accomplish their goal of discovering how college students make meaning of their ethnicity in a multicultural world. . . . The work's key strengths include a comprehensive literature review and multi-method research design. The qualitative data adds exponentially to the findings and conclusions. . . . All involved in higher education need to be aware of students' need to develop and express their ethnic identities. This invaluable resource is a must read. Summing Up: Essential."—*Choice*

"By studying the experiences of 120 Southern California college students, researchers Ortiz and Santos take an in-depth look at the role college plays in ethnic identity development. Their book provides a close look at the divergent developmental paths traversed by students of different ethnicities, and the effect college has on students' understanding of their ethnicity. With smart analysis and helpful suggestions for maximizing the positive effects of campus diversity, the volume is a significant contribution to the literature on identity, diversity, and education."—*Diversity & Democracy (AAC&U)*

22883 Quicksilver Drive
Sterling, VA 20166-2102

Subscribe to our e-mail alerts: www.Styluspub.com